Longships on Restless Seas

The History of the Vikings

Book 2

Longships on Restless Seas

The History of the Vikings, Volume 2

History Nerds

Published by History Nerds, 2022.

LONGSHIPS ON RESTLESS SEAS

First edition. November 29, 2022.

Copyright © 2022 History Nerds.

ISBN: 979-8215876039

Written by History Nerds.

Also by History Nerds

Celtic History
Ireland

Great Wars of the World
World War 1
World War 2
The Napoleonic Wars: One Shot at Glory
The Serbian Revolution: 1804-1835
Peace Won by the Saber: The Crimean War, 1853-1856
The Wars of the Roses

Irish Heroes
Grace O'Malley: The Pirate Queen of Ireland
William Butler Yeats: Nobel Prize Winning Poet
Scáthach
Finn McCool

The History of the Vikings

Vikings
Longships on Restless Seas

The Rise and Fall of Empires
Rome: The Rise and Fall

Standalone
The History of the United Kingdom
The History of Ireland
The History of America
Stalin
The Fiery Maelstrom of Freedom
The History of Scotland
Robert the Bruce
William Wallace: Scotland's Great Freedom Fighter
The History of Wales

Introduction

For centuries, a fire swept through Europe. It raged on and on, putting nations and kingdoms at its mercy, and that fire came from the North. Due to a series of socio-political triggers, the Vikings emerged from their northern homes in Scandinavia and swept all across the realms of Europe - south, east, west, and north. Mastering the navigation of the oceans and dominating the riverways, these vicious Northmen embarked upon their swift longships and introduced an entirely new chapter of Europe's history. Merciless in war and cunning in trade, they found their place in faraway nations. From Ireland, Iceland, Scotland, and Greenland, down to the Iberian Peninsula and into France, North Africa, and the distant lands in the east, the Northmen left their mark.

Some lands they ravaged, finding it a lucrative affair to extort money at sword-point. They pillaged Anglo-Saxon England, occupying parts of it and exacting tribute for several centuries before finally leaving. In the eastern lands of the Slavs, they merged with the regional tribes and became a ruling elite, establishing the realm of Kievan Rus', one of the earliest foundations of the medieval Slavic states. It was not always about war and plundering for the Vikings. They also wanted to explore new territories, establish new colonies and cultivate the land. In this endeavor, they created prosperous settlements in the Faroe Islands, Iceland, Greenland, and North America. Some of the world's earliest explorers were the Vikings: not fearing the tumultuous waves of the northern oceans, challenging the fates as they uncovered new lands beyond the edges of the world.

In the previous book, we explored the early origins of the Vikings and all the reasons why they ventured away from their homeland. We wrote of their conquest of England, their contact with the Slavs, their explorations of the far Northern shores, and their discovery of North

America. We wrote a detailed history of their most potent weapon, a tool without which their conquests would not be possible: the Viking longship. Even still, after having written all that, we didn't even begin to scratch the surface of the true history of the Vikings. Onward we go, continuing the account of their adventures and further conquests of Europe. For, as we know, wherever there was water to be sailed and shores to be found, so too, there you would find the Vikings. Now let us set sail...

Chapter 1 - The Vikings in Ireland

Last time, we offered a detailed account of the Vikings' earliest invasion, the invasion of the Anglo-Saxons. Their raid of the prosperous monastery at Lindisfarne in AD 793 is known as the earliest of all Viking raids. It opened a new era of European history: the Viking Age. Following Lindisfarne, England was subjected to centuries of attacks and extortions at the hands of the predominantly Danish Viking chieftains. News spread of new lands in the west, so the Northmen sallied forth, with new fleets of eager warriors arriving on British shores, decade after decade. Since England had neighbors, it was inevitable for the Vikings to sail along its coastlines and discover that it was not the only island within the group. In time, they also reached the shores of Scotland, Orkneys, Shetlands, Isle of Man and Ireland.

By the mid-700s, Ireland was already a nation with a long history, albeit a difficult one. For many long centuries, for millennia even, this island nation suffered at the hands of successive invaders and was ravaged by internal conflicts between feuding petty kingdoms. A country that fell under the Celtic ethnolinguistic cultural group, Ireland was a realm of fierce and proud Gaelic warriors, however poor and sparsely populated. Its inhabitants were like the land; rugged, resilient, secretive, and persevering. As one period of strife and conflict ended, a new one began. The Vikings discovered its shores and were not keen on leaving.

Upon discovering Ireland, the Vikings encountered a complex realm with many divisions. Ireland was dubbed a "complex mosaic" at the time, with roughly 150 petty kingdoms and a dozen "over-kingdoms," most of which were feuding and fighting one another. In truth, these were not "kingdoms" per se but tribal communities, called the túatha, numbering no more than a few thousand people and usually covering less than 100 square miles. These communities were best described as clans, extended kinship groups whose "kings" were the heads of old lineages. The main power of these kingdoms lay in the number of cattle they owned. Cattle in early medieval Ireland was the most prized possession of any community and a sign of wealth. Thus, cattle raids among rival tribes were widespread and the cause of many conflicts. There was a semblance of law, justice, and war leadership, dispensed by each petty king. There was also a "power pyramid" present. These petty kings owed tribute to respective over-kings, while over-kings paid tribute to a single High King of Ireland, arguably the most powerful man on the island. Yet, there were no fixed rules or an order of succession. Even a petty king could rise up, assemble a capable war band, and oust an over-king at will. Several powerful dynasties of over-kings emerged, notably the Northern and Southern Uí Néill dynasties of Ulster and Meath.

This struggling nation was full of division and looked like easy prey for the Vikings, who always had a single goal and intention. Ireland appeared to any outsider as a decentralized, unstable, and deeply divided country, which could only benefit the invader. Oddly enough, Ireland was incredibly resilient and readily absorbed the threat of the Vikings, containing their efforts to only a few highly fortified coastal enclaves and not much else. You may wonder how the Irish persevered despite this overwhelming Norse threat. The reasons were many, and the warlike nature of the Irish played a significant part in this. Even though the petty kingdoms lacked unison, with each successive Viking invasion, the Irish had warriors ready to defend whatever area was attacked.

The Irish were not welcoming of outsiders and were eager to expel them. Nevertheless, few European nations suffered as much as Ireland did at the hands of all invaders, the Vikings included. This poor island nation was one of the leading sources of slaves, commonly called "thralls" by the Norsemen. They continually raided the inland territories of Ireland, taking away poor Gaelic slaves, predominantly women, to serve their various needs and to be sold overseas. For the few centuries of Norse presence in the region, Ireland was systematically milked of its inhabitants to fuel the ever-prospering Viking slave trade, much to the dismay of its peoples. Red-haired and fair Gaelic peoples could likely be seen in realms incredibly far from Ireland, living in servitude and slavery.

The early Viking attacks on Ireland began immediately after the Lindisfarne attack in England in AD 793. However, this time, the raiders were predominantly Norwegians compared to the Danes that plundered the Anglo-Saxons. It is believed that these Norwegians sailed over directly from the southern coast of Norway and later from their bases in England. The Norwegians made stops at the Shetland, Orkney, and Hebrides Islands and wound up in Ireland, changing the fates of all these locations over the decades. Their first incursions into Ireland were small and sporadic, in a "hit-and-run" fashion. It was almost as if the Vikings were reconnoitering, getting accustomed to the lands they discovered before realizing what a ripe target for plunder it was. These attacks were generally confined to isolated and vulnerable coastal communities and remote island monasteries, which all proved ideal for raiding. The Vikings would swoop in suddenly to pillage, plunder, kill and take away slaves. They kept returning on and off for several years, roughly from AD 795 until AD 813, when there was a pause of eight years in their raids.

It is widely agreed that the first attack on Ireland occurred in AD 795, two years after the Norsemen discovered the British Isles. At that time, the band of Vikings that attacked Iona in Scotland also sailed towards Ireland and plundered a monastery on Rechru, which is likely the modern Rathlin Island off the northern Irish coast. The monastic community was ravaged, and their monastery was plundered for its riches. From this moment on, it is evident that the Vikings sailed along

Ireland's coasts, plundering their small monasteries. Inishmurray monastery was also sacked in AD 795 and then again in AD 807. The monks were slain, eventually leading to the site's complete abandonment. Further to the south, Inishbofin island was devastated in AD 795. Three years later, we hear of them again: Viking warbands attacked the east coast of Ireland, ravaging St. Patrick's Isle (Holmpatrick) and destroying the holy shrine of Do-Chonna in AD 798.

Such small and sporadic attacks along Ireland's coast continued for several years until more severe raiding began in the early 800s. In AD 836, the Norse returned and sailed up the River Shannon, plundering monasteries at Clonmacnoise and Clonfert. In AD 837, a massive Viking fleet of sixty longships appeared from the mists and sailed up the River Liffey, one of Ireland's key riverways. Sailing along it, they plundered all settlements, churches, monasteries, and other dwellings, taking away riches and slaves. It seems that this new raid was much more lucrative for the Norsemen, and from that point on, they concentrated their efforts on the east coast of Ireland, ignoring the poorer and sparsely populated western shores. Naturally, the warlike Irish clans and petty kingdoms quickly fought back, trying their best to repel the assaulting Norsemen. In AD 837, medieval Irish chronicles write that one named Saxulfr, the "chief of the foreigners," was slain at Brega by the Ui Colgain clan, but this victory was not enough. The Vikings also recognized the strategic importance of the "Black Pool," a natural harbor that today is called Dublin Bay. Here, the Norsemen set up a "longphort," a dedicated settlement that served as their wintering, repair, and assault base. This was the origin of Ireland's modern capital.

In AD 841, the Norsemen returned to Dublin in force, with one goal clearly in their mind: conquest. Like the events in England, the Norse sought to establish a permanent colony in Ireland at whatever price. The struggle that the Irish put up was not enough. The Vikings proved to be an enemy that was difficult to match. Most importantly, the Vikings had the advantage of mobility. They appeared out of nowhere, struck undefended monasteries, and escaped equally fast, unscathed. Another advantage was the rivalry and the divisions between the Irish clans. They were often unwilling to aid the affected areas of their rivals.

From Dublin, the returning Norse fleets laid waste to Western Ireland. They penetrated far inland, raiding Leinster and the Midlands, reaching as far as the Slieve Bloom Mountains. Wherever they went, the Norsemen took with them many slaves, predominantly women. In AD 845, they raided the Rock of Dunamase in County Laois and killed the abbot of Terryglass in County Tipperary. They also laid waste to many other holy sites, such as Kildare, Killeigh, Monasterboice, Duleek, Kells, Clonnenangh, Kinnitty, Swords, and Finglas. Dublin was not their only base, and in AD 845, they established a camp at Tullamore. Some Irish petty kings saw the Vikings as a valuable tool in their rivalries and wanted to use them as potential allies. To them, the Norsemen were just another element of Ireland's already chaotic geopolitical picture. As soon as the Viking raids began, bands of Irishmen also appeared who sought to take advantage of the situation to do their own raiding. The medieval Irish manuscripts describe them as plundering "in the manner of the heathens," i.e., the Norsemen.

In AD 839, the Norsemen utilized a new tactic to plunder Ireland's interior more efficiently. A Viking fleet sailed up the River Bann and into Lough Neagh. They established a fortified ship camp on the lake's shores, a so-called "longphort." From there, they raided the core of Ulster for three consecutive summers, taking away many slaves. Many longphort bases were established over the years, notably at Lough Rea, Clondalkin, Leixlip, Lough Foyle, Arklow, and elsewhere. Of course, the most important bases that were established over the decades of their raids were called Dublin (modern Irish capital), Veisafjord (Wexford), Vedrafjord (Waterford), Corcaigh (Cork), and Hlymrekr

(Limerick). These cities would last as powerful Viking-fortified naval bases and were sometimes described as "city-states." In the later years of Viking presence in Ireland, these forts would be the last Norse strongholds on the island. These permanent settlements gave the Vikings the foothold they needed to gain a tight grip on Ireland. Their permanent presence meant that they could conduct raids all year round and would not depend on the conditions of the sea. Of course, this meant they were more vulnerable now, their settlements being known to the enemy, and their sea-based mobility diminished.

One of the foremost early leaders of the Irish Vikings was known in the Irish Annals as Turgeis, which is likely the Gaelic rendition of the Norse name Thorgestr, or Thorgils. His origins are unknown; some suggest that he was a Norwegian, while others suggest Gaelic-Norse origins from the Hebrides. In AD 840, Turgeis plundered the wealthy monastery of St. Patrick at Armagh three consecutive times, burning it to the ground. This plunder was particularly difficult for the Irish. In this monastery were held many precious reliquaries and the royal treasuries of several Irish Kings. It is thought that Turgeis was the one who founded the longphort at Dublin, which would turn out to be the most successful of all Norse settlements on the island. In many ways, this Norse chieftain was one of the biggest threats and nuisances for the Irish. In AD 844, he sailed up the Shannon River, reaching Lough Ree, establishing yet another longphort camp there and raiding far and wide through the midlands. This year he plundered other monasteries, some of which were the richest in Ireland. However, in AD 845, his luck ran out. In a radical turn of events, he was captured and drowned in Lough Owel in County Westmeath by the Irish King Máel Sechnaill I (anglicized as Malachy MacMulrooney). After several decades of successful raiding, this was the first significant reversal of fortunes for the Norse in Ireland. This was also the turning point in Ireland's "Cogadh Gaedhel re Gallaibh," or "The War of the Irish with the Foreigners," the Viking period of the island's history that was penned down in the 12th century.

Either way, the Norse suffered a series of setbacks following the death of their chieftain, and the Irish gained a string of significant victories. In AD 847, the King of Osraige, Cerball mac Dunlainge, defeated the Norse at Dublin with their new leader, Hakon. In AD 848, further Norse defeats followed. Malachy MacMulrooney defeated them at Farrow near Mullingar in County Westmeath, while Olchobar mac Cinaeda, the King of Munster, slew the Norse chieftain Thorir in battle. From the early Irish annals, we also learn that in that same year, the King of Lagore, Tigernach mac Focartai, landed a significant defeat against the Norsemen in an oakwood at Disert Do-Chonna. According to the annals, over 2,000 Vikings were slain in these four battles. The annals describe the losses as "2,000 heads taken," which suggests that Irish warriors preserved the old Celtic custom of taking the heads of their slain enemies. In AD 849, these Irish successes culminated in an attack on Dublin, the major Norse stronghold. The fort and settlement were plundered and likely razed by High King Malachy MacMulrooney and Tigernach mac Focartai.

Discouraged by the series of defeats, many Norse warriors sailed elsewhere in search of easier pickings. After these events, an interesting thing happens. A new Norse fleet arrives in Dublin, numbering a massive 140 longships. However, the Irish described these as Dubgaill (the Dark Foreigners) compared to the Findgaill (the Fair Foreigners) who were there already. The distinction is likely between the Danish Vikings, who were predominantly dark-haired, and the Norwegians, who were light-haired. The annals tell us that the new expedition was led by the "adherents of the king of the foreigners," whose objective was to "exact obedience from the foreigners who were in Ireland before them." The annals also say that "afterward they confused the whole country," which is not all that hard to believe. Nevertheless, this rival group of Norsemen attacked the Dublin Vikings, slaughtering many of them. In the following year, AD 852, the Danes fought the Norwegians in a hard three-day battle at Carlingford Lough and once more won.

This confusing period of Viking-age Ireland is not that uncommon. Viking groups often had rivalries, especially between the Danes and the Norwegians. The Kings of Norway and Denmark both sought to claim parts of the British Isles for their benefit and thus sent fleets to reassert their sovereignty. Still, the Danish intervention in Ireland was relatively short-lived. In AD 853, new Viking warlords appear in Dublin, Olaf and Ivar, and they recapture the city for the Norwegians, expelling many hostile Danes. Many scholars believe their arrival in Dublin was the decisive moment in Ireland's Viking history. In Irish annals, these warlords were known as Amlaib and Imhar, and they became the first true Norse Kings of Dublin, transforming this fledgling ship camp (longphort) into an actual massive trading port that dominated the Irish Sea.

Olaf and Ivar soon established themselves as the most powerful Viking chieftains in the region. The Irish annals of the early middle ages clearly described them as "sons of King Gofraid of Lochlann (meaning Norway)," however, these origins remain somewhat obscure to historians, with several theories existing. Most historians today agree that Olaf mentioned in Irish history is Olaf the White (Óláfr hinn Hvíti), who was a sea-king of Dublin mentioned in the Icelandic sagas. He was said to have ruled jointly with one Ivar, just as the annals say. This Ivar was popularly connected with the legendary Ivar the Boneless, son of the famed Ragnar Lothbrok, but this cannot be proven. Either way, the two chieftains propelled Dublin towards prosperity and power and created a dynasty called Ui Imair (Sons of Ivar), which would be the dominant power in the Irish Sea for the next 200 years.

Chapter 2 - Dublin, Indomitable

It was inevitable that Olaf and Ivar, ruling jointly, attempted to establish a kingdom within Ireland and tried to control the various Viking factions across the island. Some of their first actions as Kings of Dublin were related to requiring tribute from all the Viking armies stationed in Ireland. At least three to four Norse factions were operating there, and the Dubliners put them under their control. Of course, it should not be surprising that Olaf and Ivar used the fragmented political situation of Ireland to their full advantage. In AD 859, they allied themselves with Cerball mac Dunlainge, the King of Osraige, against the latter's high king, Máel Sechnaill I. Cerball then campaigned with Ivar, fighting in Leinster and Munster, and then in Meath, invading the territory of Máel Sechnaill I. However, Cerball made peace with his high king and thus abandoned the alliance with the Vikings. However, this was nothing to worry about as Ivar and Olaf soon made a new pact, this time with Aed Finnliath, the Ui Neill King of Ulster. With the help of this new ally, they plundered Meath in AD 861 and 862. Máel Sechnaill I died that same year, and the Norsemen quickly turned their support to his successor, Lorcan. However, the Irish annals report that the Norsemen made a scandalous incident when they dug open the great and ancient Neolithic burial mound at Knowth, looking inside for treasures to plunder. The mound was considered an ancient pagan holy site for the Irish, and this disturbance by the Vikings was seen as a huge and insulting scandal. Soon after, Olaf and Ivar ran out of suitable allies among the Irish petty kings.

In AD 866, the Dublin Norsemen took their fleets and sailed over to Pictland (modern-day Scotland), where they raided and plundered with the help of their Norse-Gaelic kinsmen and allies. Their absence, however, was utilized by the new High King of Ireland, Aed Finnliath, who pillaged and destroyed their longphort at Ulster. He defeated a Viking force at Lough Foyle, taking 240 heads with him as trophies. Just how limited the Viking territorial control was is demonstrated by an Irish petty king plundering the Viking fort at Clondalkin, just 5 miles from Dublin, which was also looted.

From this point on, the Norse and the Irish warred bitterly. Olaf the White returned and allied with the Irish over-kings of Leinster and Ui Neill against the High King Aed. Their forces were, however, decisively crushed in the Battle of Killineer in County Louth in AD 868. One of Olaf's sons was among the fallen. Enraged, Olaf struck back in AD 869, sacking the wealthy monastery of Armagh with exceptional brutality, taking away 1,000 slaves to sell. Then, the Norsemen displayed their power when they crossed the Irish Sea and entered Strathclyde, laying siege to its capital, the Alt Clut, on the summit of the Dumbarton Rock on the River Clyde. This formidable and well-defended castle could not resist the Vikings and fell after the four-month siege. It is reported that the Norsemen returned to Dublin with a significant hoard of treasure. So lucrative was this attack that they went back to Strathclyde again, this time returning "with a great prey of Angles, Britons, and Picts," presumably slaves to sell.

In AD 872, the two chieftains were back in Meath, plundering, when Ivar died, of "a sudden and horrible disease." Olaf the White continued ruling, but death soon met him, too. He died in either AD 874 or 875, slain in battle with Constantine I of Scotland at Dollar in Clackmannanshire. However, whether this was indeed the Olaf in question remains under debate. Either way, with the two most powerful Vikings in Ireland dead, the realm entered a period of relative "peace," dubbed in the Irish annals as the "Forty Years' Rest." Without the two strong leaders, Viking activity in Ireland was significantly reduced, as Dublin became politically unstable, with a series of rulers with short-lived reigns. This period was utterly chaotic, with every ambitious Viking wanting "the piece of the cake" that was prosperous Dublin.

The first to come after Olaf the White was his son, Eystein, who reigned for barely a year. He was killed when an attacking force of Danish Vikings sacked Dublin. The Danes were likely led by Halfdan, the King of York in England, who aimed to create a vast sea-based kingdom uniting York and Dublin. The Danes were expelled from Dublin by the Irish allies of the Norsemen, chiefly Aed Finnliath, who soon placed Ivar's son, Bárðr, on the Dublin throne. The Danes returned in AD 877, but they were crushed, and their leader Halfdan was slain. After the death of Bárðr, the Kingdom of Dublin went into a rapid, unstoppable decline. Six kings followed him, all reigning briefly and without success. Then in AD 902, the Irish dealt a final blow to ailing Dublin. The two kings, Cerball mac Muirecain, King of Leinster, and Mael Finnia, King of Brega, attacked Dublin from two directions, devastatingly defeating the Vikings and sending them into exile across the Irish Sea. Historians dub this moment as the end of Ireland's First Viking Age.

Most of the "longphort" settlements inhabited by the Vikings collapsed soon after, either abandoned or outright razed to the ground by the Irish. The only longphorts to survive were those already developed into sizable towns, namely Dublin, Waterford, Cork, Wexford, and Limerick. All of these cities were established at strategic positions with excellent natural harbors. Nowadays, archeologists are attempting to deduce the exact location of the Viking settlement beneath the modern-day city of Dublin. Some finds were discovered, including warrior burials, the remains of buildings, ship rivers, and a rampart, all in the vicinity of Dublin Castle. The remains of the Norse town likely lie beneath the castle foundations, making thorough excavation nearly impossible. Still, Dublin had to survive, primarily because of its very suitable location. It had an excellent natural harbor, allowed shorter sailing distances towards Wales, Isle of Man, Galloway, and North-west England, and had all the predispositions to become the dominant port town in Ireland. It was thus ideal for Norse raiders, who could easily pillage across the region, all from Dublin. Thus it became the center of their slave trade empire.

As we learned from our previous book, the Vikings were the major slave traders of the early medieval period, mainly dealing with Slavic and Gaelic peoples. Even though Ireland was rich in gold and silver, primarily through its prominent monasteries, its inhabitants were the more lucrative prize for the Norse. The Irish population of that time was estimated at 500,000 people. Ireland enjoyed mild winters, cool summers, and reliable rainfall, allowing for plentiful grass growth and well-nourished sheep and cattle. The Irish populace was generally well-off and well-fed, and very few experienced great poverty. When slavery was considered, the Norsemen highly prized the well-to-do Irish. During the Irish Viking Age, thousands upon thousands of innocent people were taken away and sold into slavery, classed according to their status and wealth. In pre-Viking Irish society, slavery was almost non-existent and thus a novelty when the Norse arrived. In no time, the Irish warlords would take slaves during their wars and then sell them to the Vikings. These slaves were sold abroad, thousands of miles away from Ireland. Many Gaelic slaves would end up in servitude in Iceland, the prosperous Viking colony.

Even after we wrote so much, we still haven't fully unraveled the story of the Vikings in Ireland. This was one of the foremost chapters of Viking history in the British Isles. So invested were they in Ireland and the surrounding islands that many of the most famous chieftains gave their lives fighting for a piece of that maritime reward. Oddly enough, the Vikings did not have an easy job tackling Ireland. No matter how much plunder they conducted in the interior, they had no lasting successes and territorial gains, staying only on the coasts close to the sea. How? From a glance, it would seem that the Norsemen would quickly sweep over the Irish, especially with all their feuds and general disunity, but this was not the case. Anglo-Saxon England, in comparison, was quick to fall under their sway. It was divided into four major powerful centralized kingdoms, but this fact alone made England quick to topple under pressure.

In AD 865, the "Great Heathen Army of the Danes" invaded England, and the Kings of Northumbria and East Anglia were slain in battle, leading to the kingdom's collapse. The centralized rule meant simple conquest for the Norse; kill the king, topple the ruling class of nobles, and the kingdom will follow suit, and you can do all that in one devastating battle. In Ireland, this was not the case. Ireland had a wealth of petty kings, over-kings, and a High King, and they all squabbled between themselves for power and territory, no matter how small it was. The Norse thus encountered dozens of kingdoms, an equal number of kings, and many more lineages that could quickly produce new kings. Regardless of how significant an impact the Vikings had or how major a victory they won, they could not effectively topple Ireland's kings. At the same time, they could not count on any lasting peace agreement or alliance, not with so many kings to negotiate with and fight against. One would think that Ireland's many fragmented petty kingdoms could not muster enough men to fight off the Viking armies. Individually, this was true. A regional petty king was no more than a chieftain of a small tribe and could muster, on average, 300 warriors. This was barely enough to combat a Norse raiding party. However, the petty kings had to answer to their respective over-kings, and thus their forces would be combined into a larger capable army. When there are several of these to fight on a smaller territory, things become markedly different.

When estimating the efficiency of the Viking warrior in Ireland, one has to think about the opponent he is facing. The Irish at the time were still archaic in their way of fighting and, according to modern historians, could not be compared to the superior and ferocious Viking warrior. Where the latter was clad in chainmail, leathers, furs, and armed with swords, axes, and round shields, the Irish footman was usually naked, with little to no armor, armed with spears and cudgels, and wearing a small round buckler shield. The contrast is stark, but the primitive warfare of the Irish did have its positive sides. These warriors were nimble and fast and excelled in guerilla warfare and hit-and-run tactics. They had much more mobility than the Vikings, who preferred pitched fights and their iconic shield-wall tactics. The Irish would harass the Norse columns, ambush weary Vikings, and quickly disappear into the bogs and moors. It was an efficient guerilla warfare that could decimate any army over a long period. Thus, the Irish were not as easy targets as the Norsemen first thought. With the Viking defeat and their expulsion from Ireland, the Forty Years' Rest began, a much-needed period without Viking harassment. During this time, the Norsemen departed in their ships, looking for more lucrative targets, especially in England and Francia. However, around a decade later, the Franks and the Anglo-Saxons became more difficult to subdue, as they finally learned how to fight off the Vikings effectively.

In AD 914, Ireland's coasts again became an open and attractive target, offering plunder, and this time, the Vikings were back in earnest. This year, one chieftain named Ragnald, grandson of Ivar, appeared with his fleet in the waters of the Irish Sea, quickly defeating a rival Norse chief in a naval battle off the Isle of Man. He then established a formidable longphort at Vedrafjordr or Waterford. In AD 917, the brother of Ragnald, one Sigtrygg Gale (Sihtric Caech in Gaelic, likely Sigtrygg Squinty), recaptured Dublin and two years later devastated an Irish counter-attack at Islandbridge. He killed the Ui Neill High King, Niall Glundubh, and five other kings in this battle. This was a tremendous Viking victory and showed just how important Dublin was. Among the kings who have been slain were also Áed mac Eochocáin of Ulster,

Máel Mithig mac Flannacain of Brega, Mael Craibe mac Duibsinig of Airgíalla, Conchobar mac Flainn of Mide, and Cellach mac Fogartaig of South Brega. This victory allowed the Norsemen to regain their foothold in Dublin and the dynasty of Ui Imair to remain stable for the following decades.

In AD 922, another Norse chieftain, Thormodr Helgason, re-established the Norse occupation of Limerick, while other leaders recaptured Wexford and Cork. The situation was, thus, roughly as it was before the Vikings were expelled. Still, the Norse held no considerable territories except their fortresses on the coastlines. The only sizable settlement was around Dublin and was known as Dyflinnarskiri (Dublinshire). This territory extended along the coast from Wicklow (Vikinglo) in the south to Skerries (from Old Norse sker meaning a 'reef') in the north and as far inland as Leixlip (Old Norse lax hlaup meaning 'salmon leap') on the River Liffey.

Chapter 3 - The Norsemen in Wales

After the Norsemen were a formidable power in Dublin, and the whole of the Irish Sea was under their domination, they, naturally, found new targets for plunder and settlement. Wales was an inevitable stop on their path of conquest. This, however, was due to the increased Irish resistance when the Norsemen had to look for new and easier targets. Wales was, in many ways, a logical outcome. It lay just a day's sailing from Dublin or the Isle of Man and wasn't considerably ravaged by the Viking fleets. Of course, as with the rest of the British Isles, some sporadic raids occurred. The first one recorded in Wales happened in AD 852 and was followed by further attacks in AD 854 and 855. However, the Welsh were fierce warriors and fought off the invaders, killing their leader Gorm in AD 855. The land was a tough nut to crack. The warriors were fierce, the terrain mountainous, the lands poor, and the rulers powerful. When the Norse were expelled from Dublin, they were eager to give it another shot. From AD 902 onwards, their presence in Wales is noted. Still, before that, it needs to be mentioned that small Viking colonies were already present in Wales, particularly on the northern coastlines, in today's Flintshire. These settlers likely spilled over from the Wirral peninsula, just north across the river, where the Vikings already had settlements and a strong presence. Wirral today, its coasts especially, is dotted with Viking place names, such as Thingwall, Thurstastun, Kirby, Tranmere, Meols, Ness, Kirkby, Wallasey, Irby, and so on. Furthermore, there are place names in the southwest of Wales that suggest a Norse origin also, but little is known of their history.

In the mid-900s, however, Wales was ruled by the powerful leader Hywel Dda, the King of Deheubarth. His reign was long, and he was close to uniting Wales as his realm. His intentions were, however, cut short by his death in AD 950, after which Wales was plunged into a civil war between several competing petty kingdoms. This apparent weakness was a good sign for the Vikings to make their move, especially after their defeat at Dublin. A series of raids and Viking attacks began, primarily aimed at Anglesey, an island off the coast of Wales that was the closest target to Dublin. These raids occurred in AD 961, 971, 972, 979, 980, 987, and 993. One of the frequent targets hit hard was the prosperous St. David's monastery, lying on the Pembrokeshire coast. It was Wales' most important religious center but was nevertheless sacked by the Norsemen in AD 967, 982, 988, and 998 when archbishop Morgeneu was murdered. Incredibly, this monastery would be plundered at least six times until the end of the 11th century. It was a sad and unbearable fate for its monastic communities and undoubtedly a great nuisance for the rulers of Wales. The Viking raids had become so bad that in AD 989, King Maredudd of Deheubarth had to pay tribute to the Vikings at the rate of one silver penny for each of his subjects. Still, as time passed, the Viking raids in Wales were in obvious balance with their prospects in Ireland. When their power there waned and they became subject to the Irish Kings, so did the raids on Wales subside. After a while, the Vikings from Ireland were seen in Wales only as mercenaries, by this time Gael-Norse, working in the employ of Welsh kings.

In the end, it is clear that the Norse presence in Wales was somewhat limited but is still overlooked in the histories of the Viking Age. The poorly documented history of the Viking presence in this land leaves us to ask further questions and to try and piece together the puzzle of the Norse impact on the fragmented early medieval Wales. Of course, a critical piece of that puzzle are the place names of Norse origins. Many in Wales suggest that the Norse did gain at least a slight foothold in the land, both peaceful and hostile. Swansey, one of Wales' most prominent cities, has a Norse name, stemming from Sweyns Oy, or Sweyn's Island. Anglesey, too, has a Norse name, as does Skokholm Island, Freystrop, Caldey Island, Ormes Head, Stack Rock, Milford,

Fishguard, Gateholm, and others. All this serves as a vivid reminder that the Norsemen were, in fact, a known presence in early medieval Wales. However, there is no doubt that they were a minor threat to the Welsh kingdoms and had a far less active role in their affairs than virtually all other British Isle entities. As we mentioned, this has to do with Wales' unique geography, the Welch people's fierce character and uncanny ability to defend their land against invaders. As we know, the Welsh fought for centuries to maintain their independence against the Anglo-Saxons, Anglo-Normans, and the English and succeeded in the end. Not even the Vikings could subdue them, or was it instead that Wales was not such an attractive prize?

Chapter 4 - The Vikings in France and the Rise of the Normans

When the Vikings perfected their longboats with wide and functional sails, their reach was suddenly much greater, expanding far from their homes in Scandinavia. With such potent vessels, they could sail to the ends of the world if needed. By AD 793, these dragon-headed longships discovered the British Isles, and from there, it was just a question of time when they would cross over the English Channel and bridge that short distance towards the lands of the Franks, then known as "Francia." To remain faithful to the historical fact, we shall not name it "France," as it is known today, but Francia, as the world knew it back then. It is important to note that the Vikings were likely not strangers to the Franks and vice versa. Plenty of archeological evidence suggests that the Norsemen, particularly those from Denmark, previously traded and made contact with the Franks, Visigoths, and Anjevines as early as the 6th century and onwards. This was made possible predominantly through the Jutland peninsula, Friesland, and neighboring areas. Things had changed by the mid-700s, and the Norsemen were out seeking new prey. The northwestern shores of Europe, lying in Francia, were as good as those in Anglo-Saxon England.

The earliest known Viking raid in Francia occurred in AD 799, six years after the Lindisfarne attack. A marauding Norse fleet attacked a monastery on the shores of Aquitaine, but not much more is known of their attack. Similar sporadic raids likely occurred even before this, in those first decades of Norse exploratory sailings.

Just two decades later, the Vikings appear in records of Francia, as their raids became much more substantial. In AD 820, a fleet of Viking ships reached the mouth of the Seine river, but their warriors faced the

Frankish coastal guards, who repelled them. The Norsemen retreat to their boats, leaving five slain men behind. The incursions continued nonetheless, and in AD 841, a new fleet, led by the chieftain Asgeir penetrated far up the Seine River, piercing into the city of Rouen and laying waste to it. The city was plundered, and enormous amounts of loot was taken, with many buildings razed and burned. This Norse fleet then continued sailing the Seine, plundering the rich Jumiège monastery and burning it to the ground. Also, the nearby monastery of Fontenelle was assaulted and "held for ransom." The Vikings didn't sit idle. They captured 68 prisoners, likely in this monastery, and later ransomed them for a hefty payment to the monks of Saint-Denis.

Four years later, in AD 845, a new fleet appeared on the Seine. It was led by a chieftain named Ragnar, who has been identified with the legendary hero of the sagas, Ragnar Lodbrok, but there is a debate about whether they are the same person. The massive fleet has 120 ships and thousands of warriors, roughly 6,000. The Norsemen reach Paris, the capital of the Frankish Kingdom, enter the city, and lay waste to it. They take great loot, and the Franks cannot mount an efficient defense. The Vikings only agreed to leave after King Charles the Bald agreed to pay a hefty ransom of 7,000 French livres, roughly 2,570 kg (83,000 oz) of gold and silver. It was an immense sum. Yet even this is not enough. On their return voyage, they plunder other sites, including the rich Abbey of Saint Bertin. From then on, scarcely a year passed that was not marked by Norse raiding and activity. In AD 852, Asgeir and his fleet were back in action, raiding on foot, when they lay waste to the Beauvais region in Flanders from their base in Rouen. There, they are engaged by a Frankish force and have to retreat to Jeufosse Island, where they make their winter camp and control the entrance to the Seine.

However, a new group of Vikings appears. Norwegians led by Sigtrygg and Godfrid, from Ireland. They establish their base at Jeufosse, possibly commanding Asgeir and his men. A Frankish army lay siege to the island, seemingly without success. In AD 855, Sigtrygg and his fleet launched a new attack. They attempt to destroy a critical Frankish fort on the path to Paris, joined by a powerful fleet led by a chieftain named Björn. Together, they raid south of the Seine, as far as Chartres, where they come to blows with a Frankish army and suffer heavy losses. Even so, the attacks do not subside. In AD 857, the joint fleet of Sigtrygg and Björn attacked Paris and then Chartres. The latter is now seized, plundered, and almost all its populace slaughtered. Francia was currently dealing with a severe threat to its sovereignty, much like the many other kingdoms of Europe that had fallen prey to the wrath of the Norsemen.

By the following year, ever arrogant and bolstered by their victories, the Vikings continued to spite the Franks. Björn teams up with a newly arrived force of Danish Vikings led by one Hasting. Together, they led a mounted army and surrounded Paris, demanding a ransom for all the monasteries. At the same time, Charles the Bald again tries to lay siege to the Norse base at Jeufosse Island but is defeated. The defeat only gives new energy to the Norse. Around AD 859, they doubled their attacks from the valley of the Seine, where they are now a fully established presence. However, that same year, the Frankish King Charles the Bald becomes tangled in an internal struggle with his brother, Louis the German. The Vikings quickly exploited this weakness and began raiding freely from their bases. They attack and plunder Bayeux, Beauvais, Laon, and many other places, including monasteries, where they execute the bishops in several cities.

After yet another plunder of Paris, King Charles the Bald was becoming increasingly desperate, unable to deal with the lightning-fast Vikings, whose swiftness and boldness always took him by surprise. In that despair, he devised a bold plan. He offered a sum of 3,000 livres to a Viking chieftain named Veland, whose fleets were on the River

Somme. Veland, bribed, was supposed to force the Seine Vikings under Björn out of Francia. At best, it was a silly move by Charles. The plan completely backfired, as Veland and Björn came to an agreement and united their forces. However, whether all troops were united or only one part is uncertain. Either way, a few years of relative peace follow as the Norsemen go out to sea again. Charles the Bald used this period of stability to erect a series of coastal forts to control the Seine and the approach to Paris. Yet even with all these things, the Norsemen were not eager to abandon their effort in Francia. The loot was too good.

In AD 876, they came back again after a short respite. A fleet of 100 ships sails along the Seine and leaves only after taking a considerable payment from Charles the Bald of 5,000 livres. This buys a bit of peace for the Franks, it seems, as the Norsemen leave for a few years again. Next, we hear of them in AD 885, when an enormous fleet, the biggest thus far, of 700 ships sails up the Seine. Their target is Paris, which they attempt to besiege. It is now a problematic affair, and both sides suffer severe losses.

The Norse siege of Paris in AD 885-886 is one of the most significant moments in early French history. The Norsemen numbered in the thousands and were set on completely overwhelming the city. However, they were repelled, not by the inept King Charles the Fat, but by Count Odo of Paris, a powerful nobleman. The latter only had several hundred men at his disposal, but he still managed to defend the city against the besiegers. No matter what siege engines they employed, the Vikings could not pierce through the city and enter. They suffered immense casualties over several months and many attempts at entering. The siege came to an end after Charles the Fat paid a heavy ransom in gold and silver, making the Norsemen disperse and raid elsewhere upriver. Charles the Fat was considered an inept king for this, along with many other reasons. Soon after Charles the Fat's death, Count Odo was elected in his place, becoming the first king not to be of the Carolingian dynasty. In the eyes of many scholars, this is a crucial episode in French history overall. We can only imagine what would have happened if the Vikings had managed to win over Paris. However, this was only the tip of the iceberg for Norse history in Francia. The loss of life in Paris did not dissuade the Norsemen. In the worst case, they only had to wait a few years before their strength replenished and they could raid again.

Around AD 887, a new figure appears. A chieftain named Rollo is with the Seine Vikings and imposes himself as their foremost leader. Rollo is his name in Frankish rendition, but his Norse name was likely Hrolfr or Hrollaugr. We are not entirely sure, but this Rollo was likely the one who led the Norse siege of Paris, although it is more realistic that several chieftains led the siege. Either way, Rollo enters the stage in Francia, parts of which were, by this time, settled by Norsemen. After the initial incursions, people from Scandinavia began settling in the coastal regions of Northwest Francia. Especially along the River Seine, they lived in many settlements and were an established presence. Their de-facto capital was later Rouen. Today, many place names in these parts of France bear names of Old Norse origins. Examples include Dieppe, Cherbourg, Le Ham, Elbeuf, and hundreds more. Rollo was as ambitious as the previous Viking chieftains in the Seine region. He began repelling the Franks, pushing right up to the "doors" into Ile-de-France. He set his sights on the city of Chartres, where he was defeated by Robert, the brother of Count Odo. This event was almost groundbreaking. By this time, it was clear that the Vikings were an obstacle to the Frankish kings that could not be defeated. They made their homes in the coastal regions, plundered continually, and no end to the situation was in sight. A different solution was needed.

The new Frankish King, Charles the Simple, seeking to block the lower Seine, that "highway" for Viking incursions, and end the whole problem of Norse raids, made a special agreement with Rollo. The agreement was signed in AD 911 at Saint-Clair-sur-Epte, by which Rollo was granted sovereignty over the territory of the Lower Seine, which, informally, he already had in his possession for several years up to that point. The agreement also required that Rollo acts as a "shield" against further Viking incursions, i.e., that he would fight his kinsmen if they again tried to conduct raids on Francia through the River Seine. To formalize the deal, Rollo was baptized into Christianity, taking the Christian name of Robert, and married Charles the Simple's daughter (possibly illegitimate). The earliest known mention of Rollo is from AD 918, from a charter made by Charles to an abbey. The Charter mentions an earlier land grant to "the Normans of the Seine," chiefly to "Rollo and his associates for the protection of the kingdom."

Another contemporary source describes a humorous event that unfolded during these formalities, which perfectly showcases the rugged nature of the Vikings and their odd understanding of the Christian European world. As a part of the treaty signed at Saint-Clair-sur-Epte, Rollo the Viking was required to pledge his fealty to King Charles the Simple by kneeling and kissing the King's foot. At once, Rollo refused, saying, *I will never bow my knees at the knees of any man, and no man's foot will I kiss.* Instead, Rollo commanded one of his men to kiss the King's foot. The chosen Viking stepped up and crudely grasped the King's foot while he was still standing, raising it to his mouth. Naturally, the King lost his balance and toppled backward, much to the Norsemen's amusement. Still, the fealty was accepted, and Rollo gained immense power and lands. He split the land for governance among his chieftains and warriors and settled in the capital of Rouen, where he would rule. This entire episode was a significant part of European history. From the simple raids of the late 700s, the Vikings gained an ever-bigger foothold in Francia until they could no longer be expelled. They commanded a sizable chunk of land on Francia's northwest coast, eventually earning the name of "Normandy."

The name comes from "Normand" or "Norman," the name given to the Vikings by the Franks. It means, simply, "Northmen."

Rollo's land continued to grow steadily. As soon as Charles the Simple abdicated the throne in favor of King Rudolph, Rollo, in his simple Viking logic, considered that his previous deals with the Franks were null and void. Acting on this, he raided westwards, plundering yet again, causing further pressure on the new Frankish King. From this, another agreement was born, by which Rollo was given more land, Bessin and Maine. Some years later, we learn of yet another land grant, including Cotentin and Avrachin, which increased the Norse-held territories even more. Rollo died, leaving behind him his prominent son and heir, William Longsword. William, along with his son and successor, Richard the Fearless, capitalized on their predecessor's achievements and "forged" the Duchy of Normandy into one of Francia's most cohesive and formidable principalities.

In one or two generations, the Vikings were no longer purely Scandinavian. They slowly but surely assimilated into the Frankish and Gallo-Romance population, giving rise to the distinct Norman ethnicity. The Normans were much different in their customs and character than the people of Francia. By the end of the reign of Rollo's grandson, Richard the Fearless, they were said to *"have become not only Christians but in all essentials Frenchmen. They had adopted the French language, French legal ideas, and French social customs and had practically merged with the Frankish or Gallic population among whom they lived."*

The Normans were described in the 11th century as follows:

"Specially marked by cunning, despising their own inheritance in the hope of winning a greater, eager after both gain and dominion, given to imitation of all kinds, holding a certain mean between lavishness and greediness, that is, perhaps uniting, as they certainly did, these two

seemingly opposite qualities. Their chief men were specially lavish through their desire of good report. They were, moreover, a race skillful in flattery, given to the study of eloquence, so that the very boys were orators, a race altogether unbridled unless held firmly down by the yoke of justice. They were enduring of toil, hunger, and cold whenever fortune laid it on them, given to hunting and hawking, delighting in the pleasure of horses, and of all the weapons and garb of war."

The Normans were now a distinct cultural group but had much of the Viking blood in them and a love of war and explorations. Because of this, the Normans emerged as one of the most formidable groups in the Middle Ages. They established the feudal system of rule, which would later spread across Europe, and introduced many innovations into warfare and castle-building. In many ways, the Normans shaped the medieval period in Europe as we know it today. Norman adventurers continued to explore and invade throughout much of the middle ages, playing a significant part in the founding of the Kingdom of Sicily and briefly conquering southern Italy and Malta. Of course, the most famous Norman was William the Conqueror, a great-great-great-grandson of Rollo. In AD 1066, William the Duke of Normandy assembled a large fleet. He crossed the English Channel, invading Anglo-Saxon England and swiftly conquering it after winning the famed Battle of Hastings. In just 30 years, England had been transformed from the ground up, and the Normans established themselves as its rulers, eventually spreading into Ireland and across the British Islands. Undoubtedly, the Normans were a decisive factor in shaping the fate of the world as we know it today. None of that would have happened without their fierce Viking roots.

Chapter 5 - The Second Viking Age in Ireland

The Ragnald we mentioned above was seemingly not interested in ruling Dublin. Across the Irish Sea in England, York seemed to him a much better prize, so he recaptured it in AD 919. By AD 921, he was dead, and his kinsman, Sigtrygg, gave up the throne of Dublin in favor of ruling York. In his place, he set up another kinsman, Guthfrith. Dublin's new ruler adopted an aggressive stance against the Irish and launched a series of violent campaigns to ravage the countryside, plundering and taking Irish slaves. An event is recorded during this time: Guthfrith launched an attack against the wealthy monastery of Armagh, but he did it with much "respect." The monks and the infirm were spared from slaughter, and the buildings were mostly left intact. Guthfrith was likely Christian, as, by this time, the new religion was steadily seeping into the Norse ranks. Either way, Guthfrith's new piety did him no good. While returning from raiding Armagh, Guthfrith was intercepted by an Irish army led by Muirchertach of the Leather Cloaks and was heavily defeated, barely escaping.

This was a fitting start to the so-called "Second Viking Age." This meant the Norsemen could no longer freely travel the Irish countryside, plundering as they wished. Serious opposition formed and lurked everywhere. This was also established by the Irish victory over the Vikings at Carlingford Lough in AD 925 when Muirchertach again defeated them and captured 200 Vikings who were beheaded. What does this tell us about the rapid changes in Irish society? After the first invasions of the Vikings, many things were different. The Irish society became increasingly militarized, as the need for their defense was high. The petty and over-kings who could muster the most efficient men in high numbers would also receive power and prestige.

Suddenly, the Norsemen encountered more enemies who displayed a fierce resistance. Moreover, the Irish took valuable insights from the hard lessons they learned during the Viking invasions. From the Vikings, they adopted many things, including the widespread use of axes and swords. This served to tip the scales and increase the odds in their favor and against the Norsemen. There was a new viciousness in Ireland, a new and brutal way of warfare that spared no one. The natives were bitter and enraged against the invaders and showed no mercy. However, these novelties, and this new rage spread to inter-Irish warfare also. The feuding Irish petty kings did not shy away from ravaging the lands of their Irish foes and slaving their people. In the years before the Norse arrival, this was rare. This new reality in Ireland gained an altogether new character that wasn't all that favorable for the Norsemen.

Still, Dublin remained a formidable Viking stronghold. After Sigtrygg died in AD 927, his successor Guthfrith ruled it until his death in AD 934. Only his son and heir, Olaf Guthfrithson, managed to extend his grip over all the Vikings in Ireland after defeating his Norse rivals of Limerick in a fierce naval battle at Lough Ree in AD 937. Here we can also see that the rivalry between different groups of Vikings did not wane and that the rulers of Dublin were keen on creating a separate Norse Kingdom in this new land. Bolstered by his success, Olaf also teamed up with the Scots and the Brythonic Welsh of Strathclyde in one decisive attempt to defeat and win over the Anglo-Saxon York King Æthelstan, who had foiled his attempt when he was defeated at the Battle of Brunanburh. His absence and subsequent weakness after the defeat were taken advantage of by the Irish King Muirchertach, who quickly sacked Dublin in AD 938. Both of these rulers would soon meet their deaths. Olaf died after a short-lived reign in York following Æthelstan's death. He was succeeded in Dublin by Blacaire, who was an aggressive leader and an active raider. Blacaire met Muirchertach on the battlefield in AD 943, defeating him at the Battle of Glas Liathain, where the latter died. The death of Muirchertach was a great loss for the Irish, who greatly mourned him. He was described as the "Hector of the western world," and his death as having "left the land of the Irish orphaned." Of course, the rage of the Irish was immense, and they were swift to take vengeance.

The next year, the new High King of Ireland, Congalach Cnogba, descended upon Dublin, capturing and burning it. A vast amount of plunder was taken away. The annals tell us that 400 Norsemen fell in this battle, and their leader Blacaire fled into exile. Around AD 947, however, Blacaire was able to return to Dublin and reclaim his lost throne. Just one year later, alas, he died in battle and was succeeded by another member of the Ui Imair dynasty, Godfred, son of Sigtrygg. In AD 951, this Godfred swept over the Irish Midlands, plundering a string of rich monasteries, including Kells. It was a highly successful raiding campaign that yielded a great bounty. The medieval *Annals of Ulster* report, *"three thousand men or more were taken captive, and a great spoil of cattle and horses, and gold and silver was taken away."* However, it is also said that divine wrath wrought havoc on the Norse raiders. Soon after the raids, a severe epidemic erupted in Dublin, described as leprosy or dysentery, causing widespread death and illness. The Viking chief Godfred was one of the victims of this plague.

Soon after, the Dublin Vikings' power began to wane. They were no longer a viable contender for rule over York, and their threat to England diminished. Focusing on the Irish and the Anglo-Saxons was far above their capabilities. Either way, Olaf succeeded Godfred, who adopted a much calmer stance, rarely raiding unless allied to some Irish petty king. By this time, the Vikings were no longer purely Norse, i.e., Scandinavian by lineage. A distinct Hiberno-Norse (Irish-Viking) ethnicity was formed, also known as Norse-Gaels, dominating much of the Irish Sea, from Dublin and Irish coastal towns to the Isle of Man and the Outer Hebrides. After a few centuries, the Norse became fully

Gaelicized around the 12th century. Still, many Scottish Hebridean clans can trace their descent to powerful Viking chieftains, whose warlike nature remained in their blood for centuries.

After Olaf, Dublin's power was never fully regained. In AD 975, the Irish again plundered it, inflicting a heavy blow to Norse morale, as they burned the sacred pagan grove of Thor's Wood, which lay just outside the city. This was done by Máel Sechnaill mac Domnaill (Máel Sechnaill II), the new High King of Ireland. The Norsemen consolidated their forces, and Olaf Cuaran Sigtryggson, the latest Dublin ruler, summoned troops from the Isle of Man and the Hebrides to fight the Irish. This resulted in the Battle on the Hill of Tara, the sacred Irish place for the kings' inauguration. Here, the Vikings under Olaf were soundly defeated, with many losing their lives, including Olaf's son and heir, Ragnall. Olaf barely escaped the slaughter and went into exile, where he died. The ***Annals of Ulster*** describe this monumental event as follows:

"The battle of Teamhair was gained by Maelseachlainn, son of Domhnall, over the foreigners of Ath-cliath and of the Islands, and over the sons of Amhlaeibh (Olaf) in particular, where many were slain, together with Raghnall, son of Amhlaeibh, heir to the sovereignty of the foreigners; Conamhail, son of Gilla-Arri; and the orator of Ath-cliath; and a dreadful slaughter of the foreigners along with them. There fell also in the heat of the battle Braen, son of Murchadh, royal heir of Leinster; Conghalach, son of Flann, lord of Gaileanga, and his son, i.e., Maelan; Fiachna and Cuduilich, the two sons of Dubhlaech, two lords of Feara Tulach; and Lachtnan, lord of Mughdhorn-Maighen. After this Amhlaeibh went across the sea and died at I-Coluim-Cille."

The Irish decided to capitalize on this victory, besieging Dublin. The siege lasted three days and nights, after which Dublin surrendered. Máel Sechnaill II promptly released all the Irish slaves in town and imposed a heavy tribute on Dublin's inhabitants, deposing their exiled ruler. In his place, he placed a new ruler of his choosing, which undoubtedly signified the loss of Dublin's independence. Of course, as the Viking Era drew to a close across Europe, it also did in Ireland. Gone were the days of Dublin's brutal domination of Irish midlands. The kings rose against them and were now a more significant threat than before.

The end of the Vikings was evident with the rise of the O'Brien dynasty of Munster, whose famed king Brian Boru is one of the foremost figures of Irish history. Brian Boru was no stranger to the Vikings. In his earliest days, he fought them. Brian was the younger son of Cennetig mac Lorcain, the King of Dal Cais, which corresponds to modern County Clare. This king was subject to the kings of Munster. A younger son, he had little prospect of ruling, but that did not stop him from making a name for himself. In AD 967, still a young man, Brian Boru is known to have fought, alongside his older brother, at the Battle of Sulcoit, where they decisively crushed the Vikings of Limerick. As the latter fled, the Irish proceeded to plunder, sack and burn Limerick to the ground, taking away women and children as slaves and killing the men. It was the first real defeat that the Limerick Vikings experienced and was seen as a personal revenge of Brian Boru for the death of his father, who died fighting Vikings.

In time, Brian Boru's older brother won over the mighty seat of power in southern Ireland, the famed Rock of Cashel, placing the ruling family of Dal Cais on the throne. Not long after, he was murdered by the deposed king of Cashel, which now set the responsibilities to Brian Boru, the new head of the family. It was his time to prove his worth. At the same time, the exiled leader of the Limerick Vikings, Ivar, the grandson of Ivar, returned to Ireland, this time establishing a base at Scattery Island near the mouth of River Shannon. It was the tried and tested Viking tactic of their old days. Base yourself on an offshore island and raid the lands with ease, but times had changed, and Brian Boru took decisive action. In AD 977, he led his armies to Scattery Island, defeating the Vikings and killing their leader Ivar and his sons. With zero doubt, this was the end of Norse in Limerick, whose fate ended in blood and fire. The town of Limerick was now effectively the capital of Brian Boru's new kingdom. In return for their military and naval support, he allowed the remaining Norse inhabitants to remain at Limerick. Following this, Brian gradually exerted his overlordship over the remaining Viking settlements, namely Cork, Wexford, and Waterford. In time, Brian subdued the entirety of southern Ireland, eventually becoming the island's first High King, not of Ui Neill origin. He was now the most powerful ruler on the island, and the Vikings were his subjects. This included Dublin, and its Norse ruler, Sigtrygg Silkbeard. However, no ruler was left unchallenged, as Brian Boru faced several rebellions. The most serious one, of course, involved the Norsemen.

In AD 1013, the leader of Leinster, Mael Morda, allied himself with Sigtrygg Silkbeard of Dublin. The latter was Boru's subject, but they still hoped Dublin's independence could be regained. He summoned his allies: the Danish chieftain Brodir from the Isle of Man and Sigurd the Stout, the Jarl of Orkney. Their armies arrived in AD 1014. Brian Boru quickly raised an army, including his subject, Máel Sechnaill II, and a contingent of Vikings led by the brother of Brodir, Ospak. What ensued was one of the most famous battles in the history of Ireland: the Battle of Clontarf, fought on Good Friday, the 23rd of April, AD 1014, just a few miles north of Dublin. Brian Boru was in his 70s and watched the battle from afar, from his tent. Likewise, Sigtrygg Silkbeard remained in Dublin to protect it and watch from its walls. Clontarf was one of the bloodiest and most significant battles in the history of Ireland, with thousands of men fighting on each side. It lasted from sunrise until sunset and ended in the defeat and rout of the Irish-Viking forces of Dublin and Leinster. Brian Boru was again victorious, but he paid a high price. Even though he was in his tent, he was killed by retreating Vikings or by Brodir, the Dane of the Isle of Man. Also dead were Brian's son and grandson, Mael Morda of Leinster, Sigurd the Stout of Orkney and Brodir. Thousands of men were slain or drowned in the sea trying to flee. In many ways, this battle ended the conflicts between the Irish and the Vikings and the effective end of the Viking influence in Ireland. Dublin remained a prosperous town and Ireland's most important trading port, all thanks to the Vikings who founded it.

Chapter 6 - The Pagan Old Norse Religion of the Vikings

We cannot possibly write a serious book on the Vikings without mentioning one of their most fundamental aspects, their famous religion. In modern times, the Vikings have been popularized mainly through TV shows, movies, books, and "neo-pagan" movements, all of which seek to recreate the fundamentals of Norse culture. Of course, the Old Norse pagan religion is one of the foremost aspects that makes this possible. The larger-than-life tales of Odin, Thor, Tyr, or Freyr, have inspired many people worldwide, even today. The world of these deities and beings, and their magical realms, have inspired our world and seeped into some of the most familiar tales, stories, films, and books we know and love. What is especially interesting is that all this happened centuries after the Old Norse religion was largely forgotten and swept under by the onset of Christianity. Luckily, medieval chronicles penned down many aspects of these beliefs, leaving much material for posterity. Today, the Old Norse pantheon is one of the best known from the ancient world and stands shoulder to shoulder with the religion of the Ancient Egyptians or the pagan Slavs.

Old Norse religion is the most common name today, but Norse Paganism and similar titles can also be seen. Of course, we know that this is one of the branches of the Germanic religion that developed during the Proto-Norse period when the North Germanic peoples gradually became a separate branch of the overall Germanic peoples. Many of the deities and aspects of the Norse belief can be seen across the Germanic world. For the Vikings, their religion was a significant aspect of their culture and was woven into every part of their lives, from war to life in general. Sadly, no matter how strongly they adhered to it, Christianity swept over it, and the "old faith" became forgotten for centuries until relatively modern revivals. Through archeology, toponymy, written records, historical linguistics, and a lot of "deep digging," scholars and historians could perfectly recreate the bulk of this pagan religion.

The Vikings believed in a host of gods and goddesses, whose origins were undoubtedly rooted in the much older beliefs of Proto-Europeans and Proto Indo-Europeans. These gods inhabited a series of magical worlds beyond our own, where many legendary heroic tales unfolded. The gods were separated into two groups, the Vanir and the Æsir. Some sources state that the two groups waged war between themselves but stopped when they understood that they were equally influential. Thor, Odin, Freyr, Tyr, Loki, and Freya, were among the most popular and well-attested deities. Of course, the gods were not the only inhabitants of the mythological Norse world: dwarves, elves, trolls, giants, and many other familiar creatures with magical properties were also described.

There is no doubt, of course, that the Old Norse religion has deeper and much older roots. Today, it might seem magical, colorful, and at times fun, but in the distant past, it was likely much darker, with rituals unfolding that involved animal and sometimes even human sacrifice. The Old Norse religion was heavily steeped in ritual practice. Kings and chieftains had a central role in conducting acts of public sacrifice. For example, if a good outcome of war were desired, the tribe would not hesitate to offer a human life to Odin in exchange for victory. In the earliest form of the religion, the North Germanics had a deep reverence for lakes, rivers, groves, and similar places. This practice survived over many years. Today, many finely preserved items from the period have been discovered in bogs and swamps that were once lakes or ponds. They were once deposited there as ritual sacrifice. Of course, the famous bog people exist, perfectly preserved mummified human remains that were once ritually sacrificed and deposited into lakes and ponds.

As mentioned before, the religion of the Vikings was an essential aspect of their daily life, woven deeply into all of its forms, from warfare, everyday interactions, subsistence, farming, seafaring, and exploration. There were virtually no codifications of their religion, no written down set of beliefs that all had to share. Instead, the ideas were shared orally, across generations and over the lands, and were generally unified throughout the Norse world. Of course, the Vikings had no term that meant "religion" at the time. The word itself was introduced only with Christianity. How they called their beliefs, we cannot know for certain, or if they had a name for it at all. After the arrival of Christianity, the Norse referred to the preceding pagan faith as either "forn sið" (the old custom) or "heiðinn sið" (heathen custom). This suggests that they saw it mainly as a set of traditions and rituals rather than a religion, per se.

Equally important is the unity provided to the Scandinavian peoples through their shared faith and language. The Danes, Swedes, and Norwegians predominantly regarded them as a more or less unified entity, thanks to the Old Norse language they shared. Add to that the Old Norse religion, and you quickly gain a sense of cohesion and brotherly ties. Alas, this did not stop ambitious Viking warbands and fleets from fighting among themselves, as we have learned thus far in our story. The Vikings interacted with various cultures, peoples, and religions, influencing them and receiving influence from them in return. These were the Anglo-Saxons, the Slavs, the Gaels, the Balto-Finns, the Sami, and even the Inuit from Greenland. They enslaved, intermarried, traded, and fought with all these groups, and a cultural diffusion undoubtedly happened. This is why the Old Norse religion is so multi-layered. It has elements that originated in prehistory, even before the formation of the Germanic peoples, but it also has newer, post-Christian elements added by monastery scribes and bishops.

Scholars had a limited field of play when studying the Old Norse religion. It was especially odd that only a handful of runic inscriptions with religious content exist in Scandinavia, usually invoking Thor for the protection of a memorial stone. Thankfully, there exists a considerable body of literature and historical sources of Old Norse origins written in the Latin scripts, written down after the Christianization of the Norse world, particularly in Iceland, where many sagas were also penned down. One of the first and foremost textual sources on the Viking religion was the famed Poetic Edda. With other skaldic poetry, the Poetic Edda could have been composed in pagan times and only penned down by Christians. Of course, the Poetic Edda is not the only source. All the heroic sagas, the majority of them from Iceland, include at least some mentions of the religion and the deities. That is only the material that has been preserved. We can only imagine the wealth of information that has been irretrievably lost.

Often, the Old Norse religion is fittingly described as a "cultural patchwork" which emerged under many influences from earlier religions present in Scandinavia. There is, of course, no doubt that at least parts of it were influenced by the Nordic Bronze age, and the beliefs of that era. Many of the symbols and aspects of religion that appeared in the Bronze Age can again be seen in the Iron Age, during the formative years of the Nordic faith.

"In the beginning there was a world of ice and a world of fire. These collided and produced a giant named Ymir and a cow named Audhumla. The cow licked the ice and eventually revealed a man – Buri – who had been embedded in the ice. Buri married a giantess and their three grandsons – Odin, Vili and Ve – slew Ymir and from his body made the world. His blood became the lakes and seas, his flesh became the surface of the earth, his bones became the mountains, and rocks and pebbles were made from the teeth and jaws and any bones that were broken. They flung his brains into the air, and they became the clouds."

-Norse World creation story

Odin

There is no better way to start describing the Norse gods than with Odin. Considered by most scholars as the supreme divinity among the Vikings, and Germanic paganism as a whole, Odin has been attested under various different names and forms. Most of the information that is known today about this deity comes from the surviving Norse mythology, where he is associated with wisdom, healing, death, the afterlife, war, victory, battle, royalty, sorcery, poetry, battle-frenzy, runes, and death in battle. His name appears across the Germanic Pagan world in ancient times, where the name is the same but spelled differently. He is known as Wuodan, Wodanaz, Wōden, Uuôden, Wuotan, and so on. All these names likely stem from the Proto-Germanic theonym *Wōđanaz, which means "Lord of Frenzy," or "leader of the possessed." This could, again, refer to battle frenzy or the "berserk" state that many Norse warriors entered during the fiercest fights. Unsurprisingly, Odin appears throughout the recorded history of Northern Europe as a prominent and foremost of all gods of the pagans, with the earliest recorded accounts dating to the Roman Era.

"Odin (Scand.). The god of battles, the old German Sabbaoth, the same as the Scandinavian Wodan. He is the great hero in the Edda and one of the creators of man. Roman antiquity regarded him as one with Hermes or Mercury (Budha), and modern Orientalism (Sir W. Jones) accordingly confused him with Buddha. In the Pantheon of the Norse men, he is the "father of the gods" and divine wisdom, and as such he is of course Hermes or the creative wisdom. Odin or Wodan in creating the first man from trees—the Ask (ash) and Embla (the alder)_ endowed them with life and soul, Honir with intellect, and Lodur with form and colour."

In Norse culture, Odin had hundreds of names (best described as nicknames), all connected to his various roles and invocations, etc. Some of these names are Aldafaðr (father of men (or of the age/world)), Alfǫðr (Allfather, Father of All), Gǫndlir (Wand-Bearer, Wand-Wielder), Herjan (Warrior, Harrier, Lord, Leader of Hosts), and so on. One of the best sources for the various names of Odin is from the Edda of Snorri Sturluson, who compiled them with their original Old Norse names:

"Odin is called Allfather, for he is the father of all the gods; he is also called Valfather, for all who fall in fight are his chosen sons. For them he prepares Valhal and Vingolf, where they are called "einherjars" (heroes). He is also called Hangagod, Haptagod, Farmagod; and he gave himself still more names when he came to King Geirrod: Grim is my name, and Gangleri, Herjan, Hjalmbore, Þekkr, Thride, Thud, Ud, Helblinde, Har, Sad, Svipal, Sangetal, Herteit, Hnikar, Bileyg, Baleyg, Bolverk, Fjolner, Grimner, Glapsvid, Fjolsvid, Sidhot, Sidskeg, Sigfather, Hnikud, Alfather, Atrid, Farmatryr, Oske, Ome, Jafnhar, Biflinde, Gondola, Harbard, Svidur, Svidrir, Jalk, Kjalar, Vidur, Thro, Ygg, Thund, Vak, Skilfing, Vafud, Hroptatyr, Gaut, Veratyr."

In the original Old Norse rendition, some of these names would look like this: *"Saðr oc Svipall oc Sanngetall, Herteitr oc Hnicarr, Bileygr, Báleygr, Bolvercr, Fiölnir, Grímr oc Grímnir, Glapsviðr oc Fiölsviðr,"* translating to *"Truthful, Changeable, Truth-getter, Battle-happy, Overthrower, Death-worker, Many-shaped, One-Eyed, Fire-Eyed, Lore-master, Masked, and Deceitful."* As you can see, these names are various descriptions of Odin's roles in the Viking culture from every sphere. His mythical possessions and companions always accompany Odin. Geri and Freki ("The Greedy One" and "The Ravenous One") are his two guardian wolves; Sleipnir ("Slippy" or "The Slipper") is his eight-legged horse; Huginn and Muninn ("Thought" and "Memory") are his two prophetic ravens; Gungnir ("The Rocking/Swaying One") is his mighty spear; Draupnir ("The Dripper") is his magical ring that multiplies itself.

Odin was perhaps the most adored of all the Viking gods. Norse warriors heralded his name when charging into the fight, yearning for death in battle to join Odin in the afterlife in the golden halls of Valhalla. Odin was revered as a sorcerous god of all wisdom, powerful and just. In Old English texts, Odin was mainly seen as a euphemized "ancestor" of royal families, with some kings claiming descent from Odin himself. Moreover, many Germanic tribes and peoples claimed Odin as a founding figure, such as the Langobards.

"Chief of the gods is the one-eyed Odin (also known as Wodin), the god of death, war and wisdom. He traded his other eye for wisdom. With his two brothers, Odin created the nine worlds of the cosmos (universe). Midgard is the world of men, one of four worlds in the middle level of the cosmos. The other three are the worlds of dwarves, giants and dark elves. At the bottom level are the worlds of the dead, Hel and Niflheim."

Odin is described as a wise man, long-bearded and with just one eye, usually going about disguised, wearing a cloak and a broad-brimmed hat. He is said to be the son of Bestla and Borr, along with two brothers, Vili and Ve, and he is the father of the gods, notably Thor and Baldr. As the chief god, he often sought greater knowledge by obtaining the "Mead of Poetry." In this way, he provides mankind with knowledge, through sacrifice, as he hung on the world tree, upside-down, for nine days and nights, pierced by his spear. In the afterlife, he oversees the golden hall of Valhalla, where all the warriors who were bravely slain in battle will go after death, there to feast and rejoice endlessly, fighting in battle every night and resurrecting the following day. Throughout the mythic tales, Odin is accompanied by the disembodied, embalmed head of the wise man Mimir, who speaks to him in this form, speaking of the end of the world in the doom of Ragnarök and urging him to lead his fallen "einherjar" warriors into the final battle, before he is consumed by the monstrous wolf Fenrir.

Odin, by far, is the best-known of all Norse gods and has been revered by the Vikings perhaps for the longest time. In that, we can see his possible roots in the "sky father" deity of the Proto Indo Europeans and his origins far back in time. Today, the memory of Odin lives on in the name "Wednesday."

Thor

The next in line of the most famous of all Viking gods is the son of Odin, Thor. The god of thunder, lightning, storms, sacred groves, strength, fertility, virility, trees, and the protection of mankind, he is well-attested throughout Germanic history. Like Odin, he also has several names and different spellings among various Germanic peoples. In Old Norse, we know him as Þórr, in Old English as Þunor, Old High German as Donar, Old Saxon as Tunar, Frisian as Thuner, and so on. All these spellings come from Proto-Germanic *Þun(a)raz, meaning "Thunder," so the connection is pretty simple. Throughout the entire history of the Germanic peoples, Thor was documented as a highly popular god, oft-invoked and loved by all. He was depicted as strong and muscular, often red-haired and ruddy, boisterous and humorous, wielding his large and mighty magical hammer, Mjölnir. Thor's hammer is one of the six treasures built for the gods by the dwarven master craftsmen of the Norse mythological world. The Æsir considered the hammer the greatest of all the gifts because of its value. Mjölnir represented a powerful weapon against the enemy. Not only would it crush everything it struck, but it would never fail. Also, if Thor threw it at something, his aim would be true, and it would return to his hand each time. For Thor's admirers, the miniature form of the hammer became a popular amulet. People associated amulets in the shape of a hammer with Thor's role as the god of storms. In the myths, Mjölnir is sometimes identified with the thunderbolts the god was throwing. Warriors would wear symbolic Mjölnir hammers around their necks for protection and prowess.

In medieval Icelandic manuscripts, Thor is attested as having at least 15 names, much less than Odin, and a wife, the golden-haired goddess Sif. Much like his father, he too has magical companions and possessions: two servants, Þjálfi and Röskva; a magical cart pulled by two goats, Tanngrisnir and Tanngnjostr ("Teeth Thin" and "Teeth Grinder"), which he eats every night, and they resurrect in the morning; three marvelous abodes, Bilskirnir, Thrudvangr, and Thrudheimr; the magical belt Megingjörð ("Power Belt"); the iron gloves Járngreipr ("Iron Gripper"); and a powerful staff Gríðarvölr. In Norse myths, Thor is foretold to wage a fierce battle with the monstrous world serpent, Jörmungandr, during the world's end. In that battle, both would perish. Throughout history, and even today, Thor remains one of the most popular Norse gods and a source of great inspiration for the revival of Norse Paganism. Today, his name lives on in the word "Thursday."

Freyja

Naturally, not all of the deities of the Vikings were related to war, just as the Vikings were not all about fighting. These were people in connection with nature and the world around them, devoted to the land, the sea, and the mechanisms of the world. One of the foremost goddesses they revered was Freyja ("The Lady"), a deity of love, fertility, sex, gold, foretelling magic, beauty, and women. She has a brother (and male counterpart), Freyr. She presides over the marvelous heavenly field of Folkvangr, where her hall lies, Sessrumnir. She hosts half of those warriors slain in battle, sent there by Odin himself. Much like the other gods, she, too, has magical items and companions. One is her famed necklace, Brisingamen ("Gleaming Torc"); a magic cloak of falcon feathers; a chariot pulled by two cats; and a companion, a boar named Hildisvini ("Battle Swine"). Like the others, she too is attested by various names or nicknames, including Gefn, Hörn, Mardöll, Sýr, Vanadís, and Valfreyja. She is among the most frequently mentioned deities in the surviving Old Norse writings, mainly the *Poetic Edda*, the *Prose Edda*, *Heimskringla*, *Sagas of the Icelanders*, *Skaldic Poetry*, and modern Scandinavian folklore. She was invoked for fertility and love matters, primarily by mothers, wives and daughters, and by men as well. She can be seen as a benevolent mother goddess, and her roots, as such, can reach far, far back in time. She could have also been connected to plant lore and the medicinal use of plants since today, her name is associated with names of plants, especially in the south of Sweden. During the Christianization of Scandinavia, she was gradually replaced by Virgin Mary.

Chapter 7 - The Arrival of Christianity and Its Effects on Old Norse Religion

Because of the logical constraints of this book, we shall not go into detail on any other Norse deities since there are too many to speak of. Some of them include Freyr, Tyr, Loki, Baldr, Njörðr, Bragi, Forseti, Heimdall, Hermóðr, Skaði, Ullr, and others. They were, of course, the dominant aspect of all Viking and Norse lives and were the fundamentals of their culture. Most importantly, their religion was superbly strong. However, it could not endure Christianity, that strange religion from outside Europe that came and swept over the continent, converting nations and subverting cultures. The Norse peoples first encountered Christianity in the British Isles, where it was already an established and dominant faith. Also, through various trade routes, they encountered the Christians of Byzantium and the eastern lands. By the time it reached Scandinavia, it was already the accepted and established religion across Europe.

"The Christianization of the Norse countries didn't happen in a vacuum; it was part of a broader trend of Europeanization that Norse societies were undergoing at the time. Formerly, they had been part of a barbarian fringe of Europe rather than "proper" Europeans in the eyes of their southerly neighbors. But during the second half of the Viking Age, they came to adopt many of the staples of European culture and civilization, which brought them into the "proper" European fold. In addition to Christianity, these changes included the adoption of writing (beyond the nominal writing system that runes had provided), the growth of a political system based on kings rather than chieftains, and various smaller modifications of the Vikings' legal and cultural frameworks."

For rulers across Europe, Christianity was an efficient way towards centralized power. This means that with the introduction of

Christianity and the suppression of paganism, they could have a more efficient grip on the populace and greater control. This is the main reason for Christianity's quick spread and adoption across Europe. The new religion brought three things coveted by all rulers: power, wealth, and influence. Today, we don't know just how the Norsemen's conversion process was concluded, but it certainly had a lot to do with oppression and the will of individual kings. We can safely assume that Christian missionaries met with little success among the Scandinavians, so, it is only logical that the will of the influential leaders was imposed on the people until Christianity finally took root. Furthermore, the religion spread naturally throughout the large Viking world through explorations, trading, and contacts.

"The Norse judged their gods on the basis of the criterion "What can this god do for me?" (It's arguable that this is how most people from all over the world, pagan, Christian, or otherwise, have always viewed their deities, but such a question is far beyond the scope of this present piece.) The Norse judged the Christian god according to the same standard. Conversion was therefore predominantly a means of becoming convinced that the Christian god could bring more benefits than the previous gods could – or, at the very least, that he could bring enough benefits to merit being worshiped alongside the established gods. According to the traditional legends about the conversion process, missionaries often persuaded the people of the extreme power of the Christian god by performing fantastical miracles in his name, feats which always led to a great number of conversions. Needless to say, it's impossible to determine whether or not there's any historical truth in such accounts. What we can say, however, is that the Norse seem to have become convinced of the might of the Christian god largely through more down-to-earth political and economic means."

Through these contacts, migrations, and cultural exchanges, it is possible that Christianity became known to the Vikings, with some even adopting the faith. Of course, the Norsemen that settled in realms outside of Scandinavia, namely in the east, Francia or the British Isles, were gradually assimilated into those cultures and became Christians after just a generation or two. When traveling back to Scandinavia, they brought it back with them. Christian slaves, mainly from Ireland, would bring their religion to Iceland and other Nordic countries, as well, and so it spread.

In Europe, Charlemagne was one of the foremost leaders who pushed for the Christianization of Denmark. Missionaries worked there, spreading the faith, and it was in AD 826 that the Danish King Harald Klak converted to the new religion, likely due to political and economic reasons. By the time of Danish King Horik II (AD 854-867), the entire monarchy reverted to Norse paganism, showcasing that religion was likely seen as a political tool. In Norway, kings initially had a difficult time establishing the new religion. The Norwegian King Hakon the Good converted to Christianity in England and brought the faith back home. He encouraged priests to preach it and built three churches in Trondheim. They were quickly burned down as the populace was hostile towards the religion. His successor, Harald Greycloak, was also a Christian convert but met with little success in the conversion of his people. Olaf Tryggvason, a later Norwegian king, was an enthusiastic promoter of Christianity, he forced the nobles to convert, destroyed pagan temples, and killed those he named "sorcerers." This was how Christianity spread, under pressure. Neighboring Sweden was thoroughly Christian by the early 12th century. In Iceland, one of the most prosperous Norse colonies, Christianity bought trouble as the relatively small populace of the island was divided. Pagans and Christians were at odds, and an all-out conflict was a threat. After arguments at an assembly in AD 999, the Icelanders decided that the Icelandic law would be based on Christian principles but with concessions to the pagan community. Private, but not public, pagan rituals and sacrifices were allowed and remained legal. Thus, Iceland was one of the first Christian Nordic countries.

Across Germanic Europe, conversion to Christianity gained a more social aspect, as it became somewhat of a "trend" or a norm. Thus, individual conversions were almost non-existent, and mass conversion was the accepted norm. Whether those early converts understood the seriousness of the act or the monotheism of the new religion remains a matter of debate. It is known that some Norsemen found it challenging to grasp the idea of Jesus Christ and that they came to consider him just one god among many, as they were polytheistic and believed in many gods.

In time, however, Christianity erased all traces of Nordic Paganism. That is, alas, how time works, with devastating effects. Norse myths, practices, rituals, and deities remained as elements of Scandinavian folklore and not much more. With the establishment of Christianity, Paganism was increasingly condemned and demonized, and it became a taboo and a stigma. Nevertheless, elements of Norse myths survived in oral traditions, especially in rural areas, and could still be attested in the 13th century. Even those who were firmly Christian likely recounted these tales as simply amusing or historically valuable without actually believing in them. It is argued today that many Norse rulers or scholars had a revived interest in the pagan myths and tales, although remaining Christian, simply from a historiographic interest, and that because of this, Norse mythology "long outlasted any worship of or belief in the gods it depicts."

Remnants of Old Norse paganism survived in isolated pockets of Scandinavia for centuries after Christianity arrived. A notable example is the so-called Trollkyrkja, or "Troll's Church," a mountain in the heart of the National Park of Tiveden, Sweden, which served as a pagan ritual site for centuries. It was likely still in use in the 1700s when paganism was long forgotten and punishable. Moreover, the chief of the Norse gods, Odin, Thor, and Freyja, continued to appear in Scandinavian folklore until the early 20th century, especially in villages. There were documented accounts of encounters with Thor or Odin and a widespread belief in the fertility powers of the goddess Freyja. Old Norse paganism was never entirely the same again after the appearance of Christianity. It can be safely said that, with its disappearance, the age of the Vikings was finally, once and for all, gone. Luckily, thanks to the work of scholars and historians and the persevering remnants in Scandinavian folklore, a lot about the ancient Viking religion can be known with certainty and preserved for posterity.

Chapter 8 – The Norse Kingdom of the Isles

Early in the Viking expansion towards the British Isles, the Vikings gained a considerable foothold in this region. That foothold was centered on the many small islands lying off the coasts of Scotland. In many ways, these islands were the natural habitat for the seafaring Norsemen and allowed them to sail undisturbed to their other ventures in the British Isles. More importantly, these islands served as a necessary "stopgap" between Norway, England and Ireland. This foothold that the Norsemen gained in the islands would later emerge as the Kingdom of the Isles and consisted of the Hebrides, the Isle of Man, and the islands in the Firth of Clyde. It was a true maritime kingdom, perfect for the Vikings, although on a much smaller, albeit convenient, scale. Of course, these islands allowed for a connection with the Norse colonies at Shetland and the Orkney Islands, directly or indirectly connected with the Kingdom of the Isles and its history.

The kingdom existed from roughly the 9th until the 13th centuries. It was known to the Norsemen primarily as "Suðreyjar," the "Southern Isles," as compared to the "Norðreyjar" or the "North Isles," i.e., Orkney and Shetland. This entity is sometimes known in history as the Kingdom of Mann and the Isles, referring to the Isle of Man, which had a strong Norse presence throughout the Viking Age. Either way, the fate of this kingdom was turbulent, it was not always fully independent and had overlords in Orkney, England, Scotland, or Norway. Of course, this only goes in tune with the ways of the Vikings, who always competed over the choicest lands and best locations. Throughout the history of this kingdom, there was continued hostility with the rulers of Ireland and interventions of the Kings of Norway, who mostly acted through their vassal, the Earl of Orkney.

The Kingdom of the Isles was a Norse realm centered on the many islands between Ireland and England proper. The most important islands of this realm were: the Isle of Man, located in the Irish Sea, roughly halfway between Ireland and Wales; the Hebrides Islands, both Inner and Outer, of which the most important islands were Islay, Iona, Rum, Eigg, Skye, St. Kilda, Jura, Raasay, and the Firth of Clyde islands, with the largest being the Isle of Arran and Bute. Before the Vikings arrived in this area, the central place of these islands was Iona and its prosperous monastery, the center of Christianity in the British Isles. Thanks to this monastery, the region's history was well documented. Once the Norsemen appeared in AD 793, they changed everything. Soon they spread around the coastlines, laying waste to many sacred sites, Iona included. Around AD 849, the plundering became so bad that the monks had to flee Iona, taking with them the sacred relics of St. Columba. From this point on, there is a significant three-century pause in all written documents since the monasteries were largely plundered and disturbed by the Norsemen. Because of this, historians had to look elsewhere to piece together these islands' histories. Luckily, information existed in Irish, Old Norse, or Anglo-Saxon documents. Even without them, it wouldn't be hard to recognize the Norse presence and impact on these islands. The placenames there are almost exclusively Old Norse or Gaelic (to a lesser extent), and many of the words and names used daily are of Viking origins.

There is still much to be unraveled in connection with the history of this region. For example, it is not known when and how the Vikings "conquered" these islands, which were at the time a part of the Kingdom of Dal Riata. Still, it is safe to assume that the isles suffered the same fate as many other locations in the British Isles. They were overwhelmed and claimed by the Vikings. In time, however, we learn that the Vikings were quick to mix with the local populace of Gaelic origins. Much like their compatriots in Ireland, they became

Norse-Gaels, known to the Irish as Gallgaedil, the Foreign Gaels. This, in many ways, only gave them a more fierce character. The Norse-Gaels were a distinct ethnicity of mixed origins whose prowess in battle was even greater than that of the Vikings. The isles were constantly a refuge for Viking seafarers and warriors who'd come from across the Norse world. In one early source, we learn that many opponents of King Harald Fairhair of Norway fled to the southern isles to seek refuge and freedom. Whether this means that the Kingdom of the Isles was lawless and lacked cohesion, we do not know, but there are no indications to tell us this.

Harald Fairhair came to the throne in the mid-800s and was a ruthless leader. He pursued his enemies across the sea, first seizing the Shetlands and Orkney Islands for his realm and later the Hebrides. To subdue the Kingdom of the Isles, he sent Ketill Flatnose, who succeeded, but in doing so, rebelled and declared himself the "King of the Isles." After all, it seems that the position was prosperous and attractive, likely due to the strategic position of the islands that allowed for easy travel across the British Isles and thus easy access to plunder and to the slaves.

From these islands, the Vikings formally had a significant foothold in Scotland, which ushered this nation into a new age of strife. As we learned in our preceding works, Scotland had a turbulent history up to that point and was marked by near-constant warfare and inter-tribal warfare. Now, with the appearance of the Norsemen on its western coasts and isles, a new hegemony was established. This became especially evident in AD 870 when the famed Dumbarton fortress, seen by many as impregnable, was besieged and later plundered by the Vikings, led by the two brother Kings of the Norsemen, Olaf and Ivar, who arrived from Dublin. Some sources suggest that Olaf was the leader of the Kingdom of the Isles, or "Viking Scotland," and that he banded with Ivar to share the spoils of war. Still, much of the history related to the Hebrides and that part of Scotland is obscure, and it is likely that the Viking rulers of the Isle of Man also exerted influence over these isles. Little of the area is known until the rise of one Amlaib Cuaran, the next King of the Isles. His Norse name was Olaf Sigtryggson, and he likely succeeded his cousin Olaf as the King of Mann. He is recorded in contemporary sources as "Rex Plurimarum Insularum" ("King of Many Islands"), meaning that he was likely the first King of Mann and the Western Isles of Scotland. He was succeeded by the famed Maccus mac Arailt (Magnus Haraldsson), who, together with his brother, Gofraid mac Arailt, became the bane of the Irish Sea, plundering far and wide, sacking Iona, and conducting two effective campaigns against Ireland. The two are also mentioned as having won "the Battle of Man" in AD 987. By this time, they are mentioned as "King of Innse Gall," meaning the "King of the Islands of the Strangers," referring to the Hebrides. This tells us that these outlying islands have been the principal "lair" of the Norsemen and their fleets for decades.

Over the next several centuries, the Kingdom of the Isles was the site of persistent strife, as rulers of Dublin, Norway, and Scotland fought over them and the power that they brought. Norse domination persisted throughout these centuries, even though the Norse identity was in the background, as the Norse-Gaels were now a dominant group on the islands. The Norse history in the region survived well after AD 1066 and the arrival of the Normans. This left a unique character of the Hebrides and the Isle of Man, as well as the Orkneys and Shetland, where a Norse aspect can still be recognized in the folklore, culture, lifestyle, and character. Today, many of the Hebridean islands have Old Norse names, and the roots of the Viking culture can still be outlined in the character of the islanders. Furthermore, many western Hebrides clans can trace their origins to Viking chieftains. All this tells us that the modern Scottish identity includes a substantial part of Norse.

Chapter 9 - The Vikings in Spain

Within the world of the Vikings, nothing seemed impossible to achieve. The world was ripe for conquest for an ambitious Norse warrior standing at the prow of a sleek longship, with the wind of the North Seas in his hair and a sharp axe in his hand. Multiply that mindset by thousands, and you get a nation of confident and daring seafarers as arrogant as they were bold. In simplest terms, the Vikings did not shy away from any target. That is why, when studying their history, we can see their traces across the known world, from north to south. Wherever there were coasts, rivers, and seas, the Vikings sailed and plundered. It should not be a surprise that they ventured southward, towards the Mediterranean and North Africa, eventually raiding Muslim Spain and the Iberian Peninsula, where they caused great havoc and left their lasting mark. It is an exciting part of Norse history. We can only imagine how Muslim Spain, with its unique character and warm weather, looked utterly alien to the Viking raiders, who were, by that point, well used to the somber and frigid climate of Ireland, Scandinavia, and other realms.

Of course, the Vikings were equally alien to the Moors, the Muslim inhabitants of the Iberian Peninsula. They conquered much of the Iberian Peninsula in AD 711, creating their realm of Al-Andalus, which lasted for several centuries before being reconquered by the natives. The Muslims of Al-Andalus were sophisticated and unique, with their culture wholly different from that of Northern Europe. Seeing bearded, fur-clad, and fair-haired Vikings, armed to the teeth and viciously aggressive, they might have considered them like beings from another planet. Of course, the Muslims of Spain were monotheistic, being followers of Islam. They initially called the Vikings "heathens," giving them the name "Majus." This is related to "Magians," which originally referred to the Zoroastrians but came to mean "heathens" in general. Later, the Norsemen gained a more fitting nickname from the Muslims, being called "al-Ordomaniyun," related to "Lormanes," "Lordomanni," or "Normanni," all forms of the word "Northmen."

The Vikings first appeared in Spain during the reign of King Ramiro I of Asturia, around AD 844. One wandering Norse fleet approached the Spanish coasts near Gijon (Gegio) but did not attack or make landfall, considering the town was too fortified. Next, they attempted an attack near Coruna, at Farum Brigantium, but the citizens repulsed their assault. Several such raids occurred, and the city had to be abandoned. Later, King Ramiro assembled a powerful army and defeated the Norsemen in a battle near the Farum Brigantium lighthouse. The Vikings departed in their ships, and the area surrounding Coruna was freed. However, the Norsemen laid waste to the land, plundering many monasteries and leaving the region razed. The wealthy and prosperous church of San Eulalia de Curtis, nine leagues from Coruna, was utterly destroyed.

Of course, it is not surprising that the Norsemen were not dismayed by their defeat. Once back on their ships, they sailed southward along the coast, plundering and seeking an easier target. After Coruna, they reached Lisbon, conquering the city and staying there for 13 days. Next, they sailed to Cadiz, Sidonia, and Sevilla on September 25th, AD 844. The latter was the site of some fierce fighting, but the town fell to the Vikings in the end, on October 1st. The Vikings stayed there for 40 days. From then on, they would learn that Moorish Spain was not such an easy target, and resistance was met. They were in Sevilla but did not gain possession of the castle. Still, they plundered the town and attempted to burn down the mosque. An army from Cordoba was assembled and marched to meet the invaders. In the meantime, the Vikings plundered Isla Minor, Coria, Talyata, Firrich, Lacant, Moron, and other neighboring places, taking great loot. The

Muslims ambushed one of the raiding parties at Quintos-Moafir, where they were slaughtered. At the same time, the Moorish army reached Sevilla and liberated it while the Vikings fled, learning of the slaughter of one of their parties.

The Norse had to fight several more hard battles, sailing for Cadiz and Sidona and later being defeated at Talyata on November 17th, AD 844. Those Norsemen that survived sailed on to Niebla by the Tinto River, where they looted and sacked the city. Next, they journeyed to Beja, Ossonoba, and Lisbon before disappearing. Shocked and devastated, the Moors were left to deal with the damage of the Viking raids. Several cities and monasteries were sacked and left in ashes; citizens were murdered, and treasures were stolen.

The people of Andalusia were struck with fear and called the Norsemen, "enemies of mankind." They now went to great lengths to protect themselves from future Norse incursions. After all, it was inevitable that the Vikings would return, especially after tasting Spanish treasures. The people hastily built ships for defense, training sailors and assembling a fleet. People of Merida, Santarem, and Coimbra were instructed to protect the coastlines and to be on the watch for new Norsemen. This fear also spread further down the Mediterranean, and ships were busily built in Carthagena, Cadiz, and Tarragona. The flames of panic were fanned even more when the Vikings attacked Francia in AD 848. As the news of this assault spread, panic spread throughout Catalonia, which was put on alert in expectation of attacks. Many affected Spaniards considered the Vikings even worse enemies than the Moors.

This first wave of Viking assaults was just the foretaste of things to come. By studying it, we can understand that the Norsemen probably had an idea of the Iberian Peninsula and sailed there intentionally. The priests of Ireland's coastal monasteries certainly had a limited knowledge of the land lying far to the south, which likely passed on to the Vikings. Furthermore, when arriving in Moorish cities in Spain, the Norsemen could have seen Slavs as well, who, at least partly, could have seemed as "familiar faces." At the time, the Saqaliba, as the Muslims called the Slavs, constituted a significant group of slaves who often rose to prominent positions in al-Andalus. Many slaves were imported into Spain from the Frankish Empire, poor souls captured in Denmark, Saxony, and among the Polabian Slavs. Perhaps some of them sought their freedom among the invading Norsemen. Either way, this tells us that Moorish Spain was a multilingual nation, and it is likely that once there, the Vikings had no trouble making themselves understood, as is agreed by several leading scholars.

As was suspected, the Viking raids were soon to continue. Asturian King Ramiro I died in February of AD 850 and was succeeded by his son, Orondo I. In AD 859, Orondo faced a major Norse invasion. A massive fleet of Viking ships attacked Galicia and Asturias, laying waste. The expedition was possibly led by two famous Norse chieftains, Bjorn Ironside and Hastein, as contemporary sources state. Either way, the Norse raids began in earnest. Their fleets moved from Galicia (coasts of present-day Portugal) to the mouth of Guadalquivir, the Raya region, Cartama, Malaga, la Raduya, and the area of Ronda. Wherever they landed, the Norsemen pillaged, laid waste, took slaves, burned mosques, and took great loot. From here, the tremendous Norse expedition of Bjorn Ironside continued to Djezirat-al-Khandra and Algeciras and onto the coasts of North Africa, where they landed in Mauretania (in modern Morocco) and fought a hard battle against the Berbers. There, they penetrated the city of Nacchor (modern Nekor), taking away many slaves later sold in Ireland. After this, they left Mauretania, returning to Spain, landing at Todmir on the coast of Murcia, this time on the peninsula's east coast. They pillage again, defeat the locals, and take the Castle of Orihuela. From here, the

Vikings made several raids inland, allegedly reaching as far as the French border.

Next, the Norsemen take Pamplona by surprise and capture its King, García Íñiguez. The latter had to pay a hefty sum of 90,000 denars to be released. Next, the Norsemen sailed to the Balearic Islands, raiding Mallorca, Menorca, Ibiza, and Formentera. From there, they sailed into the mouth of River Tech (on the modern border between Spain and France), plundering the wealthy Roussillon monasteries there. Afterward, they settled on the island of Camargues at the Rhone estuary, their winter base. Even from here, they raided Valence, Nimes, and Arles. When spring came, Camargues was abandoned, and Bjorn Ironside and Hasting sailed on to Italy, where they destroyed Pisa and plundered Luna. By AD 862, they were back in Brittany on the coasts of Francia. From there, they possibly went back to their homes.

As we can see from this lengthy account, the Viking expedition in the Mediterranean was nothing short of an absolute success. Wherever they sailed, the Vikings plundered without mercy, taking a large amount of loot and several slaves. Undoubtedly, the so-called "Mediterranean Expedition" of Bjorn Ironside and his associates significantly augmented their fame, wealth and power. All the coasts of Iberia were seriously affected, as we read. The expedition lasted no more than a year, but its effects were profound. The populace of both Muslim and Christian Spain felt its consequences for years to come. The new kings did all they could to fortify their cities against new invasions, and the people feared the vicious Northmen. Such was the merciless nature of the Vikings. Of course, this was not the last Viking assault in the Mediterranean. However, it was not conducted by Bjorn Ironside or any of his contemporaries. This is perhaps due to other political and economic events that unfolded elsewhere in the Viking world. Roughly a hundred years passed before the Norse were again near the Spanish coasts. This time, they were not in such great numbers as before, but even so, their attack was now the most threatening of all.

In AD 966, the King of Leon, Sancho the Fat, died and was succeeded by the five-year-old Ramiro III. In AD 968, when Ramiro was seven years old, a powerful Viking fleet numbering 100 ships landed in Galicia, led by King Gudrød.

"In the second year of his reign (Ramiro III, i.e., 968), one hundred ships of Vikings (Normani) with their king Gundered penetrated the cities of Galicia and with much slaughter in the lands of Santiago, whose bishop Sisnando perished by the sword. They sacked all Galicia as far as the Pirineos montes Ezebrarii. In the third year of their settlement, God, from whom nothing is hidden, brought down his vengeance upon them; for just as they had carried the Christians away captive and put many to the sword, so many ills fell upon them until they were forced to go out from Galicia. Count Guillelmus Sánchez, in the name of the Lord, and with the aid of the Apostle Santiago whose lands they had devastated, went out with a great army and, with divine aid, killed all the pagans, including their king, and burned their ships."

Who this Gudrød was cannot be said with certainty, but he was nonetheless a man of power, as he could lead a fleet of 100 ships. After landing in Galicia, they went towards Iria, plundering and razing all villages along the way. They moved towards St. Jago de Compostela, where they pillaged the entire region, slaying the bishop there. Unopposed, the Vikings under Gudrød spread across the countryside, reaching as far inland as the Cebrarian mountains between Leon and Galicia. Here, they stayed for a whole year. However, they now had to face a massive Galician army led by Count Gonzalo Sanchez, who defeated the Vikings, slaying King Gudrød. After this, the Norsemen made no more substantial attempts at raiding Iberia with seriousness. After AD 969, just a few minor Viking attacks were recorded, in AD

984, 1016, 1018, and 1050. Even though Gudrød's expedition was far less successful than that of Bjorn Ironside, it was nevertheless more threatening for Spain, partly because of the state of the kingdoms at the time. Had Gudrød done things differently, the outcome of his expedition could have been much more dangerous than it was.

"The Viking voyages to Spain were primarily of the reconnaissance and plunder category, but some trade occurred as well. The Vikings did not stay as long in Spain as they did in for instance France and the British Isles because of the distance and because of the fact that Spain was more densely populated than these areas. The Vikings characteristically left a country as quickly as they entered it, preferably on the great rivers which were an important part of the infrastructure. The rivers made it easy for the Vikings to come and go as they pleased."

The Vikings never made any permanent settlements in Spain or elsewhere on the Iberian Peninsula. The raids in this region are perhaps the most iconic portrayal of what the Vikings truly were. They were ambitious and bold raiders, pirates in the truest sense of the word, who wanted nothing more but to fight and take the loot. The devastating expedition of Bjorn Ironside is one of the most memorable episodes of the Viking Age. They managed to loot and pillage countless cities, monasteries, and villages in just one year, thanks to their lightning-fast tactics and unparalleled approach to raiding and fighting. After shedding so much blood, stealing so many treasures, and setting aflame entire cities, they were back in their longships, wind and sea salt in their faces, with zero regard for the lives they took or the injustice of their raiding. After all, theirs was the world in which only the strong survived.

Chapter 10 - The Vikings on the Caspian Sea and the Journeys of Ingvar the Far-Traveled

While the Viking world in the west was full of turbulent ups and downs, conquest, bloodshed and feuds, the world in the east was somewhat different. The Vikings, who mixed with and ruled over the Slavic tribes, came into contact with various cultures and languages. As they were known in the east, the Rus' were now in contact with the Khazars, the Volga Bulgars, different Finnic and Slavic tribes, Turkic tribes, Caucasian tribes, the Byzantines, and many other tribes. The Vikings that established a ruling caste among the Slavs emerged as a prosperous and powerful entity, slowly creating the foundations of the Kievan Rus', a vast trading emporium that dealt in various commodities, of which slaves, furs, and pelts were the most common ones. Even though these "eastern Vikings" slowly became Slavic in all aspects, the Viking blood still ran through their veins. That meant raiding, exploration, and battle were still primal urges. Just as the Vikings of the west raided and explored far and wide, so did the eastern Vikings. Even though they had no seas or oceans to sail on, they utilized all rivers and waterways, and even overland portage routes, to reach new and faraway lands and seek fortune there. The Rus', between AD 864 and 1041, conducted a series of expeditions to the east, reaching the Caspian Sea and causing havoc among the various peoples living on its shores.

These "Caspian expeditions" are best described as military raids, which the formative state of Kievan Rus' undertook for political reasons, but also as independent raids with a simple aim: plunder. The Caspian Sea and its shores housed a variety of ancient cultures and civilizations in today's Azerbaijan, Dagestan, and Iran. The Rus', of course, already had knowledge of these people, or at least some part of them, since one of their trade routes, the Volga route, passed "close" to the Caspian shores. The Norse name for this faraway eastern land was "Serkland." Some sources claim that the name is cognate with Saracen (a common medieval name for Muslims), thus meaning "Land of the Saracens," or is connected to Old Norse "serkr" (shirt), meaning "The Land of the Gown Wearers."

The first Viking raids in the region occurred from AD 864 and into the late 800s. Likely, these were independent Viking raids on a small scale, which left no lasting impact on the area. The first one we know of occurred during the reign of Hasan ibn Zaid, ruler of Tabaristan, sometime after AD 864. The Vikings attacked the eastern shore of the Caspian Sea at Abaskun but were repulsed. In AD 913, the first major Viking incursion in the Caspian region occurred. A mighty fleet of 500 ships ravaged the Gorgan region (modern-day Iran) and raided further to the west, in Gilan and Mazandaran. Getting there, however, was no easy task. The Vikings had to pass through the Khazar lands. They promised the Khazars half of their spoils to do that peacefully. Next, they sailed down the Dnieper River, entering the Black Sea, and then into the Sea of Azov. Afterward, they sailed into the Don River past the Khazar city of Sarkel and then by portage (overland route upon which they carried or rolled their ships) into the Volga River, which allowed them to enter into the Caspian Sea.

In this epic raid, many treasures were plundered, and several slaves were taken captive. Baku was raided, as were Arran, Tabaristan, Beylagan, and Shirvan. However, the success of this fleet was short-lived. Upon their return, the eastern Vikings were attacked (likely ambushed) by the Khazars in the Volga River Delta, where many were slain. Those that managed to flee were primarily decimated by the diverse tribes in the middle Volga River Basin region. Because of this loss, there came a pause in raiding for some 30 years.

The next expedition occurred in AD 943 when a new Viking fleet captured Bardha'a, the capital of the ancient state of Arran, which was located in modern-day Azerbaijan. Again, great plunder and treasures were gained through this raid. The Vikings stayed in the city for several months, during which many inhabitants were slain. After a while, a bout of dysentery broke out among the Rus', and they had to leave the city and return to their lands. A contemporary Muslim writer, Ibn Miskawaih, speaks of this episode as follows:

"the Rus' indulged excessively in the fruit of which there are numerous sorts there. This produced an epidemic among them . . . and their numbers began thereby to be reduced."

This bout of dysentery was disastrous for the Rus' Vikings. Seeing their weakened state, the expelled people of Bardha'a attempted to recapture their city. A battle ensued in which the weakened Vikings lost 700 warriors and barely escaped encirclement. Soon after initiating a retreat to the fortress, they were besieged. They only managed to save themselves, sick and exhausted, when they *"left by night the fortress in which they had established their quarters, carrying on their backs all they could of their treasure, gems, and fine raiment, boys and girls as they wanted, and made for the Kura River, where the ships in which they had issued from their home were in readiness with their crews, and 300 Russes whom they had been supporting with portions of their booty."*

The next documented attack of the Rus' Vikings was more of an organized military expedition rather than a miscellaneous raid. It happened in AD 965 and was led by the famous Sviatoslav the Brave, Prince of Kiev. It was an expedition aimed at defeating the lasting enemy of the Rus', the Khazars. Sviatoslav commanded a great Rus' army, bolstered by Oghuz Turkic and Pecheneg mercenaries. The Prince of Kiev had great success: he devastated the Khazar city of Sarkel, razing it to the ground. Also demolished was Kerch, and later, in AD 968, the Khazar capital of Atil was burned to the ground. It was said in ancient sources that Sviatoslav's wrath was exceptional and that these cities were wiped out of existence, with not even a leaf of grass remaining. With this victory over the Khazars, the Rus' gained a firm hold on the north-south trade routes, entirely altering the region's demographics and tilting the power levels. In the following decades, Viking raids in the area continued, albeit on a smaller scale.

The area of the Caspian Sea is essential in the overall history of the Vikings, even though they were, by this time, well known as Rus', or "Slav-Vikings." The reason for this importance was the enduring conflict between the Rus' and the Khazars. One of the foremost reasons for the animosity between these two states was likely the dominance over the Volga trade route since some of it passed through the Khazar state. Naturally, they collected duties for the Rus' goods transported down the Volga River. Let's keep in mind that the Volga was quite important for the Rus'. Through it, they transported their precious honey, furs, pelts, and slaves down to the markets of Byzantium. Other reasons included Byzantine incitement, Rus' raids, and the Khazar blocking of the Volga. As we mentioned, it was Sviatoslav of Kiev who brutally laid waste to the Khazar state, abruptly ending the ongoing conflict with it.

With that final Rus' victory in the Caspian Sea region, one would think that the raids would end. Much was yet to be plundered, and many cultures and civilizations of the region remained independent and untouched. This was known to the Vikings, and that meant further expeditions. In the late 980s and early 1000s, small-scale and sporadic Viking raids in the area occurred without lasting effects. It wasn't until AD 1042, and the expedition of the famous Ingvar the Far-Traveled, that the Vikings left one of their last impacts on this remote region. Ingvar assembled a massive fleet of 200 longships, carrying up to 20 thousand men, and led them to the far east.

This exploit of Ingvar was later penned down in Iceland by a monk in the famed saga called *Yngvars Saga Viðförla*. The saga describes what would become the final expedition of the Vikings into the Caspian Sea region. One Ingvar, the Far-Traveled, a Viking explorer from Sweden, launched the journey. There are indications that Ingvar was connected to some Swedish nobility, but his identity remains unknown. He assembled a substantial fleet in Sweden and sailed east, into the land of his kinsmen Rus', and from there to the Volga and into the Caspian region. The exact purpose of this expedition is also uncertain. They could have sought to raid and seek treasures, as did the Rus' before them.

Another possible reason was the reopening of old trade routes, mainly because Bulgars and Khazars were no longer an obstacle. Ingvar managed to gather 30 ships for his endeavor. His crew was Icelanders, Swedes, Rus', and possibly Norwegians and Danes. Either way, not much is known historically about Ingvar's expedition. Upon reaching the region, Ingvar likely entered the Georgian King Bagrat IV's service. On his side, the Vikings fought in the Battle of Sasireti in AD 1042. It is known that a detachment of 1000 Vikings ambitiously charged the enemy before any order was given. The move proved disastrous, and the battle was a major defeat. Ingvar and many of his men were captured, and many were slain. The rest of the expedition was a disaster with no gain. Those men that were not killed in battle were now plagued by disease. Many lost their lives due to this sickness, including Ingvar the Far-Traveled. This was the end to his fame and travels: of the 30 ships of his expedition, only one is reported to have returned to Sweden.

Today, no less than 26 runestones mention Ingvar's expedition. Of these, 23 are located in the Lake Mälaren area in the Uppland region of Sweden. This tells us that most of Ingvar's warriors (and likely Ingvar himself) began their journey from this area. The runestones were raised posthumously for warriors that never returned from the Caspian region. Almost all the runestones tell of death found in the east with Ingvar. This expedition is an essential insight into Norse raids and explorations. It tells us that not all of them were successful, as we learned before. Sometimes the idea panned out. Bjorn Ironside laid waste to the coasts of Iberia and the Mediterranean, gaining unimaginable wealth and influence with minimal losses and obstructions. Ingvar the Far-Traveled, however, met with nothing more than death, disease, and misfortune on his expedition.

We learn that the Norsemen were not always victorious during these expeditions. They had to ensure the endeavor's success and the odds needed to be in their favor. Ingvar likely thought to recreate the success of past Viking expeditions to the Caspian Sea area but failed to take into account the uncertainties of the far eastern lands. Still, the Norse spirit was unshakable. The Vikings did not ask about the distance, danger, or ferocity of the enemy they faced. To them, no obstacle was impossible to overcome, they accepted any task and battle unless it was clear that victory was unattainable. The Vikings did not fear death in battle nor death in an exploratory raiding expedition. For them, it was an expected entry point into Valhalla, where Odin presided. Without question, young Vikings rushed to join Ingvar's retinue and went far to the east only to die. At home, parents and siblings, uncertain of their ultimate fate, raised runestones to preserve their names for posterity.

Chapter 11 - The Viking Age in Estonia

For most of their history, the Vikings had a special relationship with Estonia and the other neighboring lands of the Baltic coasts. For thousands of years, the shores of the Baltic Sea were home to some genuinely fierce people. Like the Vikings, they were people of the sea, honed by the harshness of the frigid waves and shaped into a hardy and persevering people. They were the diverse Slavs of Pomerania, the Baltic Curonians (Kurs), whom even the Vikings feared, and then the Estonians, further to the east. All of these people were in the Scandinavian sphere of influence. The Baltic Sea was like a great round table. At one end were the Swedes and the Geats from Scandinavia. At the other end were the Danes. In between, there were the many seaside Slavic tribes, along with the Balts, Estonians and others. The sea united them all. They all "ate" from that same round table, the Baltic Sea. Arguably, the most robust culture was the Scandinavians or the Vikings. Their culture influenced all the others, and in some cases, they intermixed. It was well-known in history that Polabian and Pomeranian Slavs shared centuries of cultural ties, but the others were not so welcoming.

The Curonians of modern-day Latvia and Lithuania were noted as such ferocious seafaring warriors that even the Vikings feared to clash swords with them. In fact, throughout history, the Curonians raided Swedish shores and warred with the Norsemen. Then there were the Estonians. At the time of the Vikings, Estonia was a region of loosely allied tribes. Those nearer the coasts of the Baltic were largely under Norse cultural influence, especially those living on the two large islands off Estonia's coast: Saaremaa and Hiiumaa. To the Vikings, the land was known as Estland (or Eistland, Esthland), and the entire region as Austrvegr (The Eastern Route). Beyond it lay Gardariki (The Realm of Towns), the land of the Rus'. The largest island of Estonia is Saaremaa.

In Viking times, it was called Ösel, and its inhabitants were Oeselians. These peoples had a long history with the Norsemen and are attested in the Old Norse Icelandic sagas as *Víkingr frá Esthland*, or *Vikings from Estonia*. In all regards, they were Vikings: their trade was seafaring, war, and piracy. They were not, however, ethnically the same. These were likely the speakers of a Finnic language like Estonians are today. Nevertheless, they were Vikings in all but speech. Remember that "Viking" is not an ethnicity but a calling.

These Vikings from Estonia shared many similarities with the Norsemen. Ancient chronicles mention them as seafaring people, dependent on the waters around them (they were islanders, after all). They used special sleek warships, very similar to those the Vikings used. These elegant ships had special dragon head prows and rectangular sails and excelled in speed and maneuverability. Because of this, the Oeselians were skilled raiders, up to par with the Swedes and Norwegians. These people are also reported worshiping "Tharapita" or "Taara," a powerful god that is comparable to Norse Thor. No matter how similar to the Norse they were, their relationship was not always ideal. For the most part, the two cultures were constantly at war, raiding each other's coasts, plundering, and taking away slaves. The island of Saaremaa was of particular interest to the west. It is the one island frequently mentioned in Norse sagas, where the Vikings likely had moderate presence and lasting pretensions. Early in the history of the Viking Age, we hear about conflicts between the Vikings and the Oeselians of Saaremaa. In the famous Icelandic *Njal's Saga*, we learn that a vicious battle between these two people occurred off Saaremaa in AD 972. However, the Viking Age in Estonia did not begin in AD 793, as it did in the rest of Europe. In Estonia, it is likely to have begun around AD 800 and ended around AD 1050 due to several factors, which we will mention later.

Saaremaa, and much of ancient Estonia, was dotted with hillforts and fortified cities. During the Viking Age proper, many places on Saaremaa evolved into heavily fortified towns, likely due to the increased threat from the Norsemen. Many Viking fleets sailed to Estland for their summer raids, especially prior to the 700s, before the rest of Europe became a more lucrative target. Many prominent chieftains and even kings are mentioned in that regard. For example, the famed Snorri Sturluson writes in the *Ynglinga Saga*, about the Swedish King Ingvar from the 7th century AD, the son of King Östen, and a great warrior of his age. During his time, the Swedish Kingdom was under constant threat from the Estonian Vikings who plundered its shores. In response, Ingvar invaded Estonia, achieving moderate success at first, but later losing a battle against a massive Estonian army. He lost his life in the process and was buried on the shores of that eastern land.

Another recorded event mentions the arrogance and the ferocity of the Vikings from Estonia. It tells of the Norwegian Queen Astrid Eiriksdottir, who fled internal conflict in the realm in AD 967, seeking refuge in the lands of the Rus'. However, en route, she and her son were kidnapped by these Vikings from Estonia and made into slaves. Six years later, the queen's brother, Sigurd Eiriksson journeyed into Estonia, and by chance spotted the young boy in a slave market at Saaremaa, whereupon he recognized him and paying for his freedom. This boy was Olaf Tryggvason, who would later become the King of Norway. From this account, we can understand that the Estonian raiders were particularly ferocious and cared little for whom they were looting and kidnapping. They prowled the Baltic Sea like hungry wolves, embodying that true Viking spirit which they shared with the Scandinavians.

For ages, however, Saaremaa was a veritable battlefield between the Norse and the Oeselians. It is possible that some amount of settlement was made by the Vikings, especially on the coasts and in the southern Sõrve Peninsula. Several Nordic Iron Age ship burials were discovered in this area, dated to AD 700-750. The fight for the island should not be strange, mainly because it was the wealthiest of all Estonian regions in ancient times. The Norse wanted a piece of that land, but the fierce Estonian Vikings were hard to tackle. They raided each other back and forth for centuries: in the Chronicle of Henry of Livonia, we learn that a fleet of sixteen Oeselian warships, probably in the late 900s, ravaged the coastal areas of southern Sweden. We also know that in AD 1000, a Viking raid on Saaremaa (known to the Norsemen as Eysýsla) occurred. This latter event is described in Icelandic *Njal's Saga*, dealing with the exploits of Gunnar Hamundarson, who fights in that raid. The saga tells us the following:

"Thence they held on south to Denmark and thence east to Smálönd and had victory wherever they went. They did not come back in autumn. The next summer, they held on to Rafala (Tallinn) and fell in there with sea-rovers, and fought at once, and won the fight. After that they steered east to Eysýsla (Saaremaa) and lay there for a while under a ness. There they saw a man coming down from the ness above them; Gunnar went on shore to meet the man, and they had a talk. Gunnar asked him his name, and he said it was Tófi. Gunnar asked again what he wanted. "Thee I want to see," says the man. "Two warships lie on the other side under the ness, and I will tell thee who command them: two brothers are the captains—one's name is Hallgrímur, and the other's Kolskeggur. I know them to be mighty men of war; and I know too that they have such good weapons that the like are not to be had. Hallgrímur has an atgeir (a special spear) which he had made by seething-spells; and this is what the spells say that no weapon shall give him his death-blow save that atgeir. That thing follows it too that it is known at once when a man is to be slain with that atgeir, for something sings in it so loudly that it may be heard a long way off—such a strong nature has that atgeir in it."

Back and forth, the raids went on. Century after century, the two cultures of Vikings raided one another. The Danish medieval chronicler, Saxo Grammaticus, writes in his **Gesta Danorum** that in AD 1170, a fierce battle happened on the Swedish island of Öland. At the time it belonged to Denmark: the Danish King Valdemar I had to mobilize his entire fleet in order to push back the vicious raiders from Saaremaa and Kuronia. Even centuries before, Öland was targeted by the Estonians, as early as AD 600. This tells us of the lasting feud between the two nations, and their warlike Viking nature that simply would not let the matter rest. One of the last raids of the Estonian Vikings occurred in AD 1187, when they are mentioned in the **Eric Chronicle** as having raided the Swedish town of Sigtuna. The heathens from Estonia burned the town to the ground, killing the Archbishop of Uppsala in the process. It was a shocking event, especially considering that the Estonians were among the very last pagans in Europe at the time which was long after the Norsemen had adopted the Christian religion, and their age of plundering ended.

Nowadays, we can get substantial glimpses into the Viking Age in Estonia, mainly through archeology. Saaremaa especially is the site of numerous discoveries from the Viking Age, belonging to both the Norse and the Oeselians. A number of individual and communal ship burials have been uncovered, and the swords, weapons, items, and jewelry discovered in them are all common to the Scandinavian and North European trends of the Viking Age. Undoubtedly, the most famous was the discovery of the Salme ships in 2008 and 2010. Salme is a village on Saaremaa island, which saw great Viking activity. The Salme ships are the classic clinker-built Scandinavian longships dated to the Nordic Iron Age. They were used for two separate ship burials, likely around AD 700-750. The first burial contained the remains of seven individuals, while the second had around 35 skeletal remains. Altogether, the remains of approximately 42 individuals were discovered, as well as six dogs, two hunting hawks, and assorted weaponry and funeral items. Most of these individuals were males, aged between 30 and 40, and killed in battle. Their skeletons showed several wounds typical of Viking Age conflicts. Genetic analysis shows that almost all came from central Sweden and met their demise in Saaremaa in Estonia. These were likely Viking warriors, fallen in one of the battles with the Oeselians. Also, DNA analysis showed that four of the men were brothers, and were related to a fifth man, possibly their uncle. One can only imagine the tragedy of four brothers falling in battle in distant Estland. The smaller ship of the two was used for the burial of 7 men, while the larger one contained the other 35 skeletons buried in four layers. Detailed examination of the ships concluded that they were likely built between AD 650 and 700 in Sweden and were already used for decades, patched and repaired, before finally being used for burials. The examination also revealed that the ships used sails. This is an important discovery, making the Salme ships the oldest known vessels to use sails in the Baltic Sea region. Besides the men, six dogs were ritually sacrificed and buried, and two hunting hawks, likely to serve the fallen warriors in the afterlife. Besides this, numerous grave goods were deposited with them: fragments of more than 40 Viking swords were found, and almost all were bent out of shape to prevent looting. Also found were remains of spears, shields, numerous arrowheads, an ax, knives, sharpening stones, a bear-claw necklace, whalebone gaming pieces, a bone comb, and similar odds and ends.

Over the years, scholars have interpreted these burials in various ways. The most common interpretation is that these were Norse warriors who had fallen in a Viking raid on Saaremaa. This, however, puts into question the exact start of the Viking Age, which before was considered to have begun in AD 793 with the Norse raid on the Lindisfarne monastery in Anglo-Saxon England. The supposed attack at Saaremaa took place between 50 and 100 years before Lindisfarne, pushing the date further back. Moreover, there is evidence that this was a major raid and that several buried warriors were of noble birth. Many of the swords were of exquisite craftsmanship with expensive bronze hilts. Another theory is that this burial contains the remains of Ingvar, the warring prince from the *Ynglinga Saga*, whom we mentioned in Chapter 10. He was reported to have fought against the Estonians and perished on one of his raids, being buried in Estland.

That the Vikings conducted numerous raids in Estonia is further established by a number of recovered runestones all across Scandinavia, that were erected for warriors fallen in Estland and the Baltic area in general. There are at least 15 such runestones, many of them situated in the area of Uppland. One, for example, is raised in memory of Anundr, who fell in Virland in Estonia. Another stone, from Västergötland, speaks of Olafr, "a very good valiant man," who was killed in Estonia, or Æistlandum in Old Norse, and so on, and so on.

Eventually, the Viking Age in Estonia came to a much-needed end, primarily due to several factors. As the centuries passed, the Estonian Vikings abandoned life in fortified settlements, and villages increased in number. Coastal areas that were most threatened were now fortified and well protected. Also significant is the rise of centralized authority in Estonia. All this meant that the Vikings no longer saw it profitable to raid Estland, the risks were too great, the danger immense, and the gains didn't pay off. In Scandinavia, Christianity overtook Old Norse paganism, and the rise of kings and a feudal system marked the final end of the Viking Age. From there on, the fate of Estonia changed entirely. Nevertheless, the story of the Vikings from Estonia cannot be overlooked from the overall story of the Viking Age, as it tells us that the Vikings were not exclusively Scandinavian, and that this lifestyle spread throughout the Scandinavian sphere of influence.

Chapter 12 - The Vikings and the Islamic World

Throughout the history of the Viking Age, the Norsemen excelled as seafarers and explorers. Their voyages led them to faraway places, which likely seemed utterly alien to them. If you thought that Ireland, Spain, Byzantium, or Iceland was exceptionally distant, think again. The Vikings did not stop there. They went even further, reaching Baghdad. At the time, one of the centers of the Abbasid Caliphate and perhaps one of the largest and foremost of the world's centers of learning, Baghdad was a very advanced city, on par with the greatest imperial capitals of Europe. It was a multicultural hub, a center of art, culture, and learning, filled with different nationalities and religions. We can only imagine the cultural shock the Vikings received upon reaching Baghdad.

Journeying there was not a regular practice since the trip was more than 5,000 kilometers. The Norsemen had to sail the rivers of the Rus', eventually reaching the Caspian Sea, which had to be crossed. From there, they would travel on camels to Baghdad, where they hoped to sell their wares. This city is one of the few where the Norsemen did not raid or cause trouble. Here, they were simply traders from a distant land. They indeed stuck out with their appearance, language, and customs. It was a true clash of cultures. Let's back up for a moment and remember that the Vikings were not the only ones who traveled extensively. Most of that era's geographers, chroniclers, and travelers belonged to the Islamic world. Many of these scholars emerged from Baghdad and explored the European world, which was alien to them. They left some very important writings to show us glimpses into the life of that era.

These Islamic explorers traveled on several occasions to the lands where the Norsemen lived. Most of the time, this was the Kievan Rus', where the Slavs and Vikings intermixed into a singular culture. They also connected with the Norsemen in other parts of Europe. They had a collective name: "saqaliba," meaning "Slavs," but used for all Europeans with a ruddy, fair complexion and that distinctive Norse appearance. The most famous of all the Islamic travelers was Ahmed Ibn Fadlan, who provided the most accurate and descriptive writings on the Norse. There were also other scholars to write of them, such as Muhammad al-Idrisi (AD 1100-1165), al-Muqaddasi (AD 940-991), Ibn Khordadbeh (AD 820-910), al-Mas'udi (AD 896-956), Ibn Rustah (10th Century), al-Tartushi (AD 1059-1127), Miskawayh (AD 932-1030), Ibn Hawqal (10th Century), Ibn Qutiya (10th Century), Yaqut al-Rumi (AD 1179-1229), Yahya Ibn Hakam al-Bakri (AD 772 – 866), Ibn al-Athir (AD 1160-1233), and Ahmad al-Ya'qubi (AD 897-898). Without their writings, our picture of the Norsemen would essentially be incomplete.

Interestingly, their observations of the people that they found so alien are only sometimes kind and unbiased. The Muslims of that time lived a distinct lifestyle, and the rugged ways of the Norsemen seemed to them incredible in so many ways. *"They are the filthiest of all Allah's creatures,"* writes Ahmad Ibn-Fadlan blatantly. *"They do not purify themselves after excreting or urinating or wash themselves when in a state of ritual impurity after coitus and do not even wash their hands after food."* Then again, he goes on to write that he has *"never seen more perfect physiques than theirs – they are like palm trees, are fair and reddish, and do not wear the tunic or the caftan."*

Still different, however, is the account of Ibn Rustah, who writes:

"They keep their clothes clean, and the men adorn themselves with armbands of gold. They treat their servants well and dress exquisitely

because they are such keen traders... They are generous to each other, honor their guests and treat well those who seek refuge with them, and all who come to visit them. They do not allow anyone to annoy or harm them. And whenever anyone dares to treat them unfairly they help and defend them."

As we see, the accounts of the Vikings are often conflicting. The Islamic scholars were confused: most of the Norsemen were dressed exquisitely. They displayed strong bonds of honor, an emphasis on gold and jewelry, and an unmistakable character of generosity and indulgence. They also did not observe the practices that Muslims found mandatory: they did not wash in purification after excretion, urination, or intercourse. They were likely boisterous and accustomed to alcohol and pork (both of which Muslims do not consume) and would often have intercourse freely with their slave-girls in front of one another. These things were undoubtedly cultural shocks to Muslims, and thus they wrote about it with such disgust. Ibn Fadlan was shocked after observing one custom, and he penned it down thus:

"Every day they must wash their faces and heads and this they do in the dirtiest and filthiest fashion possible: to wit, every morning a girl servant brings a great basin of water; she offers this to her master, and he washes his hands and face and his hair, he washes it and combs it out with a comb in the water; then he blows his nose and spits into the basin. When he has finished, the servant carries the basin to the next person, who does likewise. She carries the basin thus to all the household in turn, and each blows his nose, spits, and washes his face and hair in it."

This interesting ritual does sound vulgar from a 21st-century perspective, and it was undoubtedly odd for the Muslims. For the Vikings, it could have been a ritual of bonding and mutual respect, a unique way of showing unity and brotherhood with their brethren. Take, for example, long voyages on the sea, where a crew of roughly 30 men would share the cramped longship for days and weeks on end. In such an environment, one man depended on another, and brotherhood was everything. They also had to share everything, including the water with which they washed their faces. This symbolic sharing of the bowl could reflect that and display unwavering honor and brotherhood. The Islamic traveler found it repulsive. This does not mean that the Vikings were filthy or unhygienic. On the contrary, they were notably focused on their excellent appearance, much more than some contemporary cultures. For example, in Anglo-Saxon chronicles, invading Danes were described as paying great attention to their looks. They carried special bone and antler combs, with which they often groomed their hair and beards to look tidy and presentable. They sported various unique hairstyles, wore stylish clothing, and all men wore jewelry and arm rings, displaying their allegiance and wealth. Also, they bathed often, having a particular day of the week that was for bathing.

Throughout their contact with such various civilizations, the Vikings also encountered different religions. Among the Irish and Anglo-Saxons, they encountered Western Christianity. Among the Byzantines, they met with Eastern Christianity. In Baghdad and al-Andalus, they found Islam. Among the Slavs, they met various new gods, and in Greenland, they met mysterious natives. All these cultures wanted to influence the Norsemen and introduce them to their respective religions. The Vikings remained true to their Old Norse gods for a time. After several centuries, leading Norse kings toyed with the idea of becoming a part of one of these religions. The Muslims, through their contacts, attempted to introduce the Norsemen to Islam. One interesting anecdote mentions that Prince Oleg of the Rus', a Norsemen through and through, said to several foreign representatives to describe their religions to him, so he could consider converting. When hearing out the Islamic representative, he at once stopped him when hearing that Muslims do not consume alcohol. The Norsemen were fond of mead, beer, and other drinks, so Islam at once was out of the question. In time, the Norsemen adopted Christianity, but long after Oleg's time.

We should not doubt that at least some of the Vikings who traveled abroad became Muslims. The Muslim geographer, Amin Razi, mentions that *"...they (the Vikings) highly valued pork. Even those who had converted to Islam aspired to it and were very fond of pork."* According to him, at least a few of the Norsemen became Muslims. It is a fact that they had knowledge of Islam. Arab silver dirhams are among the most common archeological finds in Scandinavia and across Europe since they were the staple in the eastern trade routes and of exceptional worth. However, one archeological find puts the Norse knowledge of Islam into a new perspective. The discovery of a woman's grave in Birka, some 25 kilometers west of modern Stockholm, was unexceptional in most regards. In it was found an exquisite silver ring with a polished gem. The gem had a carved inscription in Arabic letters: "il-La-La," or "to Allah. How did such a ring end up in Sweden, and to whom did it belong? Birka was one of the foremost Viking towns and a significant trading emporium. There is no doubt that it was the home of Norsemen who journeyed far to the east, perhaps as far as Baghdad. Was the ring a simple trinket? Or a symbol of one's Islamic faith? We may never know for certain, but the ring, and the finds of many Arabic silver dirhams across Germanic Europe, tell us that the trading connections between the Islamic world and the Norsemen were not as superficial as one would think. In any case, we can thank the Golden Age of the Islamic world in the Abbasid Caliphate for the wealth of information that they left to us concerning the Norsemen and the Kievan Rus'.

Chapter 13 - Viking Towns and Trading in the Viking Age

It is wrong to think that the Vikings were warriors and raiders who loved nothing more than pillaging and enslaving people. They did love that, but it was not their whole endeavor. Remember that Viking is a calling. To go "Viking" is to go raiding. Norse people generally excelled in seafaring, trading, bargaining, negotiating, exploring, and setting up new colonies. They were skilled farmers and artisans, and their trades helped them excel in the commercial world of the Viking Age. Because of this, it is worth dedicating a few lines to the major Norse towns and the trading of the Viking Age. After all, these Norse towns were the centers of Scandinavian culture, they were major trade emporiums where different cultures and languages mixed, and trade flourished.

Among the most famous Nordic towns were Birka, Reric, Hedeby, Odense, Århus, Roskilde, Helgö, Sigtuna, Aldeigjuborg (Ladoga), Gnezdovo, Holmgarðr (Novgorod), Kiev, York, Dublin, and so on. In most of these towns, Vikings were not the only inhabitants. They were actual melting pots of diverse cultures. Thanks to the Norse explorers who brought back exquisite and sought-after goods, trade flourished in them. Much of the sea-based trading was made possible thanks to the Norse cargo ships, which were wide and had a good carrying capacity. The Slavic "lodias" inspired such ship designs, specially built cargo vessels for navigating rivers and the Baltic Sea.

Some of the listed towns were reserved only for local, short-distance trade. At the same time, some grew into major centers that attracted merchants from faraway places, such as the Arab states, Byzantium, and even Asia. After all, the Norse often dealt with goods that were not available in other parts of the world and that furthered their wealth and prominence. The Vikings gained access to such goods primarily thanks to their explorations of distant edge-of-the-world places. For example, from Vinland, they gained access to quality timber. Byzantium provided imported precious goods such as silk, spices, wine, gems, jewelry, brocade, fruits, and silver. They brought walrus ivory, furs, wool, and skins from Greenland. Iceland supplied them with abundant fish, animal fat, wool, clothing, sulfur, and falcons. They acquired most of their slaves from Ireland. They brought tin, honey, woolens, wheat, barley, silver, and linen from England. From the Slavic lands of the Rus', they acquired plenty of slaves, as well as furs, wax, pelts, and honey. They found fine weaponry, jewelry, wine, wool cloth, salt, and glass in Francia. The Shetland Islands imported soapstone and fish. They had access to timber, iron, whetstone, tar, and barley in Norway. Sweden produced plenty of iron and furs. Lastly, they found slaves, furs, fish, and plenty of precious Baltic amber in the Baltic lands. As we can see, the Norsemen had access to a wealth of precious goods in their Viking world.

Even with all this, little is known in detail about the trade in the Viking Age. Undoubtedly, most surviving accounts of their trade are from Icelandic sources, thanks to the law books that survived. It is likely that most Norse merchants were far from professional traders: they were above all farmers and seafarers, more used to the sword than to the merchant's scales. The Norse trader almost never sent a representative, instead, he himself conducted the trade, which was mostly done through barter. The most successful traders, of course, were those who possessed a trade ship that they could sail to different cities and realms. Those that did not have that luxury, had to be passengers and were allotted a certain amount of cargo space to transport their goods. When these traders sailed to faraway places, they naturally did not return at once. A journey began in summer, the crew stayed at their location in winter, and then returned back home in spring. Since the dangers were too great, sailing in winter was usually not practiced. The greater the distance, the longer the voyage. We can safely assume that some Norse traders would not return home for several years, but once they did, they came back noticeably richer. Baghdad, as we mentioned, was the farthest place the Norsemen went for trade, and journeying there was an immense feat.

One of the most popular trading destinations was, however, Byzantium, and the imperial city of Constantinople, known to the Vikings as "Miklagarðr," the Great City. Constantinople was at the time one of the largest cities in the world, and being the Byzantine Empire's capital, it attracted people from all sorts of cultures and civilizations, and was a melting pot of different influences, gathering people from the Far East, Asia, Africa, and Arabia. Of course, its markets were bustling and full of various goods, but primarily slaves. It would certainly pay off for Norsemen to make that long a voyage and sell their wares there. Trading in the Viking Age was usually accomplished through barter.

The medium of exchange was silver, which could be in the form of coins, unworked rods of silver, or in the form of jewelry. The value of this silver was based solely on its weight. Norse traders utilized weight sets and bronze scales with which silver was weighted. If a given piece of silver was more than the needed weight, it was cut up into smaller pieces in order to complete the transaction. The cut-up silver was known as "hack silver." Today, many of the uncovered hoards of precious items contain rough and random bits of hack silver, which although crude and shapeless, possessed value. During the earlier part of the Viking Age, most of the silver in circulation had its origins in the Arab world and found its way to Northern Europe through what is now Russia. Towards the end of the 10th century, the prosperous silver mines near Baghdad were running dry, and this shifted the sourcing of silver all the way to central Germany and the silver mines in the Harz Mountains.

Throughout the Viking Age, some Norse realms became prosperous. Of course, you already know all too well that this wealth was not entirely made by trading for bits of silver. Most of it was due to raiding and plunder, dealing in slaves, and receiving payments from foreign Kings. Such payments were made to the Viking raiders so they would leave a foreign nation in peace. The most famous of these payments were called "Danegeld" and were made in Anglo-Saxon England. They occurred elsewhere in Europe, also. It is estimated that at the end of the 10th and the beginning of the 11th century, in the course of just 25 years, the English paid the Danes a whopping 150,000 pounds (68,000 kilos) of silver. One can only imagine the mind-boggling weight of silver and gold that the Vikings acquired throughout the Viking Age. A modern study shows the approximate exchange rate of silver in that period. For example, eight ounces of silver equaled four milk cows, 24 sheep, or 72 meters of homespun wool, while 12 ounces were enough to purchase one adult male slave. Remember that one ounce of silver equals roughly 28-30 grams and that the standard silver coin of the Norse era weighed just a bit over 1 gram (0.04 ounces). The Arabic dirham, for example, weighed more, perhaps more than double that, and was thus highly sought-after by the Vikings.

That's that in regard to the trade in the Viking Age world. From these lines and hard facts, we can understand that the Vikings were much more than simple raiders and pirates. Wherever they found themselves they managed to establish prosperous colonies and cities that quickly turned into major regional centers. Upon their arrival in Ireland, for example, the Vikings created some of the first cities, and dominated the region in commerce and naval supremacy. They did so elsewhere too, in York and in the Rus' lands. This gives us a much deeper insight into the character of the Vikings, telling us that they were skilled traders, businessmen, navigators, barterers, colonizers, and much, much more.

Chapter 14 - The Varangians and the Byzantine Guard

No matter how powerful, the Eastern Romans and their vast Byzantine Empire still had to encounter the wayfarers from the distant north, the Vikings. To the Byzantines, they might have seemed just like countless other "barbarians" living on the empire's fringes. They soon discovered that the Vikings were much more. That they would quickly become a serious threat to the already frail Byzantine Empire. The name "Varangians" was given to the Norsemen by the Byzantines and was known in Old Norse as Væringjar, Medieval Greek as Varangoi, and Old East Slavic as Varyazi. The name applied equally to warriors, settlers, explorers, and traders, whose origins were primarily in Sweden. These Swedes eventually formed the Medieval state of Kievan Rus', a competitor to Byzantine supremacy and a formidable power that united the East Slavic Tribes. Today, scholars are trying to piece together the puzzle of the name "Varangians." It likely comes from the Old Norse word "væringi," a compound of the words "vár" (pledge) and "gengi" (companion). Thus, the meaning would be something along the lines of "sworn companions" or "confederates." According to modern sources, the literal meaning would be "a foreigner who has taken service with a new lord by a treaty of fealty to him."

The word "væringi" has cognates in other Germanic languages of the time: in Old English as "wærgenga," in Old Frankish as "wargengus," and in Langobardic as "waregang." Also, as cognates are Old Norse "foringi," meaning "leader," Old English foregenga, and Gothic "fauragaggja," meaning "steward." All these words roughly have the same connotation, referring to the leadership role that the Vikings assumed over the warring Slavic tribes in the east. There is also substantial evidence that these Varangians, or the Rus', were not entirely separated from their homelands in Scandinavia. Many later returned home after many years of service and exploration. The most substantial evidence is in Viking runestones, which were raised across Scandinavia. Those stones that refer to the Varangians or the Byzantine Empire are primarily scattered in modern-day Sweden. The stones were often raised in memory of fallen warriors whose bodies remained far away in a foreign land. Many such were in service to the Byzantines as mercenaries and thus died fighting the empire's wars. These stones also mention voyages to the East (Austr), mainly through the Eastern Route (Austrvegr). They mention Garðaríki (modern Russia, Ukraine, and Belarus), as well as Langbardaland (Italy), as well as Grikkland (Greece, i.e., Byzantine Empire).

The Varangians gained most of their fame through their service in the Byzantine Emperor's guard. The Norsemen were highly valued as skilled warriors that rarely met their match in the east. As such, they were perfect for the needs of the Byzantine Emperor, whose life was almost always in danger. However, the members of the Varangian Guard likely suffered significant losses fighting for the Emperor, as evidenced by many a number of the "Grikkland" runestones. Some of these, however, were raised by Varangian warriors who eventually returned home. There is no doubt that they returned from the east with significant influence from the Byzantine culture. They likely adopted the fashion style, the speech, and the customs. They would've brought back exquisite goods never seen in their small Scandinavian villages and were likely very rich after years of service. Several excavated Viking Age graves in Sweden and across the Viking world displayed luxury items that likely originated in Constantinople and beyond the borders of the Byzantine Empire.

The earliest Byzantine written record of the Rus' Vikings was penned down before AD 842, quite early in the Viking Age. That observation is found in the *Life of St. George of Amastris*, where a Norse raid in Paphlagonia is recorded. Another mention of them is located in the

Annals of Saint Bertin, mentioning a delegation from the Byzantine imperial court to the Frankish Emperor Louis the Pious at Ingelheim in AD 839. In the Byzantine delegation were also two men called "Rhos" (Rus'), who were different in appearance. The Frankish King inquired about their origins and learned that they were Swedes. Alas, Louis, the Pious was wary of them, thinking they were spies for their kinsmen Danes (with whom Franks warred), thus imprisoning them.

Throughout the history of the Rus', attacks on Constantinople were documented. The empire's heart was undoubtedly an attractive prize for Norse raiders, and they did not shy away from trying to penetrate it and take its riches. Such was the boldness of the Vikings. One of the first such attacks occurred in AD 860 under the Viking brothers Askold and Dir, based in Kiev. These early attacks were somewhat crude initially, as the Vikings harried their enemies, sailing in crude Slavic monoxyla down the Dnieper River and into the Black Sea, where many Greek colonies were waiting. As the Vikings gained more support from their Scandinavian brethren and the Kievan Rus' began to take shape, more extensive raids took place. Among these were raids in the Caspian Sea region in the AD 870s, AD 910, 912, 913, 943, and much later. The relations between the Byzantines and the Kievan Rus' were largely peaceful and focused on extended trade. Still, this did not stop the Vikings from repeatedly launching attacks on Constantinople, threatening the empire's capital every few decades. One such expedition occurred in AD 907 and then in AD 941. At that time, the Rus' Prince Igor besieged Constantinople but was defeated when the enemy poured fire on his ships, decimating his ranks. The Rus' also raided territories outside Constantinople, such as the AD 968-871 invasion of Bulgaria in the Balkans, by the famed Rus' leader Sviatoslav the Brave. In AD 1043, another raid was recorded when Yaroslav the Wise sent his son Vladimir to attack Constantinople, an assault repulsed with significant losses.

Still, some of the Vikings from the East found themselves in the retinue of the Byzantine Emperor. These men were known as the Varangian Guard, or "Tagma ton Varangon." This was part of the Byzantine Army and the elite personal bodyguards of the Byzantine Emperors from the 10th all the way to the 14th centuries. Initially, the guard was primarily composed of Varangians from the Kievan Rus'. Later, the Vikings from Sweden, and sometimes from Denmark and Norway, were the dominant part of the guard. They were easily recognizable in the Byzantine Court, they wore luxurious and exuberant clothes, in many colors and with rich details, they carried distinct Viking weapons, usually sported long hair and odd hairstyles, and long beards and mustaches. Many of them were blonde and ruddy. One source states that the Swedes usually carried rubies in their ears, which was also a method of distinction. Over the centuries, the life of the Varangian Guards was very adventurous and also had the promise of wealth and fame. Because of this, many of the young men from Sweden sought to embark on such a life and emigrated to the Byzantine Empire. So great were the numbers of these men that there was a medieval law in Sweden's Västergötland region, called the Västgötalagen. The law declared that no man could inherit anything while staying in "Greece" (Byzantine Empire), in a bid to stop such massive emigration. Still, many Scandinavians found themselves in Byzantine employment, seeking fame and wealth through martial prowess.

Across the European world, there are extant remnants of the Norse adventurers that belonged to the Varangian Guard. For example, on one of the high balconies of the famous Hagia Sophia, at one time the largest Christian church, a Norse name is carved as a graffito. The runes spell out the Viking name "Halfdan" and were likely carved by a bored Varangian guardsman posted in the church at one time. The runes can still be seen today. Another graffito was found nearby, also in Hagia Sophia, and possibly reads "Arí," another Viking name. The Norsemen, naturally, brought their own traditions with them, wherever they went.

One of these traditions was to carve runes in memory of their fallen brethren, and whenever stones were not readily available, they found other solutions. One such is the runic carving on the so-called "Piraeus Lion," an Ancient Greek lion statue that was once housed in the port of Athens (today it is situated in Venice). A group of Varangians made an elaborate carving on the sculpture, displaying a traditional curved lindworm, and inside is a runic inscription. The translations are uncertain, with one proposal claiming that it reads as follows (on the right side of the lion):

"Asmund cut these runes with Asgeir and Thorleif, Thord and Ivar, at the request of Harold the Tall, though the Greeks considered about and forbade it."

Another inscription on the left side reads:

"Hakon with Ulf and Asmund and Örn conquered this port. These men and Harold Hafi imposed a heavy fine on account of the revolt of the Greek people. Dalk is detained captive in far lands. Egil is gone on an expedition with Ragnar into Romania and Armenia."

Today, the runes are barely visible, due to years of natural erosion.

The Varangian Guard was composed chiefly of Norsemen from Sweden and elsewhere for the first hundred years. After the Norman conquest in AD 1066 of Anglo-Saxon England, many members came from Anglo-Saxons and "others who had suffered at the hands of the Vikings and their cousins the Normans." Many of these men were warriors and minor noblemen who lost their lands and masters during the Norman invasion of England and thus sought employment elsewhere. The mixed ranks of Norsemen and Anglo-Saxons was an even more efficient fighting unit since the Anglo-Saxons already possessed a shared link with the Norsemen from the preceding centuries. Thus, a tradition of faithful and oath-bound service developed, emphasizing honor and brotherhood. The Varangian Guard excelled in warfare and protected the Emperor, and fought in Byzantine wars and battles, where they were often the deciding factor. By the late 13th century, however, the Varangians were primarily assimilated into Byzantine culture and society, and Scandinavian elements slowly faded. Still, the guard was an active military unit until the middle of the 14th century. A contemporary record from AD 1400 still lists some people identifying as Varangians long after the end of the Viking Age.

Conclusion

Alas, no matter how successful and influential the Vikings were, their age was bound to end. In many ways, it ended as abruptly as it began, and the period of Norse supremacy ended. There were several reasons why the Viking Age ended. Most importantly, the nations once ravaged by marauding Norse fleets were now well aware of the threat and successfully consolidated to fight the Vikings wherever they were. Many of the territories traditionally raided by the Vikings no longer made an easy target, and the risks greatly outweighed the rewards. By the early 1000s, a triumphant return from a raid was no longer guaranteed, and there were many more ways to die than to get rich. Also, by the 11th century, united kingdoms were established in Denmark, Sweden, and Norway, significantly reducing the Viking lifestyle. Of course, one of the most important contributors to the end of this age was the establishment of Christianity and its rapid spread through Scandinavia and the rest of Europe. The new religion united the Norse countries under a single Roman scepter and also pacified the nations. With Christianity, new laws were also introduced. New kings and rulers were adopted through legitimacy and traditional lines of succession rather than through violence and battles, as was the rule during the Viking Age. The states became organized, which meant higher living standards, a complex bureaucracy, and complex laws and societies. The younger sons of minor nobles now had greater chances of making a name for themselves and did not have to go "Viking" to plunder and kill to do so.

On the other hand, the Vikings that lived for generations in foreign lands were gradually assimilated into those societies and lost their Norse identity. With all these things combined, the Viking Age lapsed into relative obscurity, and the Vikings were no longer at the center stage of European events. The raids stopped, and the Norse countries entered under the fold of the rest of Christian Europe, as was inevitable. With that, the Old Norse religion, the traditional Viking way of life, and other cultural traits of the Norsemen, gradually disappeared and were forgotten. The year AD 1066 is commonly taken as the end of the Viking Age, which began in AD 793. It is because AD 1066 was the year of the Battle of Stamford Bridge when the Norwegian King Harald Hardrada was defeated during his invasion of Anglo-Saxon England and killed alongside most of his Norse warriors. After this, things were never the same. Still, elements of the Vikings survived for centuries after, one way or another. Their heritage was part of the culture of the Normans, who were instrumental in the fate of Europe for centuries after. They were also in the blood of the Gallowglass warriors, who were also employed as mercenaries across Europe.

Simply put, the Vikings left such a long-lasting mark on the world, that in many ways they shaped its destiny. We can only imagine how the world would look today were it not for them. Or more interestingly, how would the world look if their age lasted for centuries more? Either way, the Vikings deserve both our loathing, and our admiration. Loathing for all the bloodshed they made, on warriors and innocents alike, and our admiration for all the feats they achieved, and new lands they discovered. After all, many of us today feel great inspiration when recounting the tales of the Norsemen: their lives of seafaring, ambition, exploration, discovery, warfare, and mythology are exciting even today, many centuries later.

By Aleksa Vučković

References:

Bruun, P. 1997. *The Viking Ship*. Journal of Coastal Research, 4.

Brøgger, A. W. 1951. *The Viking ships, their ancestry and evolution.* Dreyer.

Christys, A. 2015. *Vikings in the South: Voyages to Iberia and the Mediterranean.* Bloomsbury Publishing.

Downham, C. 2007. *Viking Kings of Britain and Ireland: The Dynasty of Ívarr to A.D. 1014.* Dunedin Academic Press.

Evans, A. 2008. *Iceland: The Bradt Travel Guide.* Bradt Travel Guides.

Esposito, G. 2021. *Armies of the Vikings, AD 793–1066: History, Organization and Equipment.* Pen and Sword Military.

Greenling, J. 2016. *The Technology of the Vikings.* Cavendish Square Publishing.

Gregory, D. 1881. *The History of the Western Highlands and Isles of Scotland 1493–1625.* Birlinn.

Hall, R. 2010. *Viking Age Archaeology.* Shire Publications

Hall, R. 2012. *Exploring the World of the Vikings.* Thames & Hudson.

Hinds, K. 2010. *Vikings.* Marshall Cavendish.

Hjardar, K. 2018. *Vikings.* The Rosen Publishing Group, Inc.

Haswell-Smith, H. 2004. *The Scottish Islands.* Canongate.

Hunter, J. 2000. *Last of the Free: A History of the Highlands and Islands of Scotland.* Mainstream.

Jóhannesson, J. 2014. *A History of the Old Icelandic Commonwealth: Islendinga Saga.* University of Manitoba Press.

Jones, G. 2001. *A History of the Vikings.* Oxford University Press.

Kendrick, T. D. 2012. *A History of the Vikings*. Courier Corporation.

Mark, J. 2019. *The Legendary Settlement Of Iceland.* Ancient History Encyclopedia.

McCoy, D. 2012-2019 *The Vikings' Conversion to Christianity*

Scheen, R. 1996. *Vikings raids on the Spanish Peninsula*. Complutense University of Madrid.

Various. 2005. *Viking Empires.* Cambridge University Press.

Don't miss out!

Visit the website below and you can sign up to receive emails whenever History Nerds publishes a new book. There's no charge and no obligation.

https://books2read.com/r/B-A-ODOK-ZSEDC

BOOKS2READ

Connecting independent readers to independent writers.

Also by History Nerds

Celtic History
Ireland

Great Wars of the World
World War 1
World War 2
The Napoleonic Wars: One Shot at Glory
The Serbian Revolution: 1804-1835
Peace Won by the Saber: The Crimean War, 1853-1856
The Wars of the Roses

Irish Heroes
Grace O'Malley: The Pirate Queen of Ireland
William Butler Yeats: Nobel Prize Winning Poet
Scáthach
Finn McCool

The History of the Vikings

Vikings
Longships on Restless Seas

The Rise and Fall of Empires
Rome: The Rise and Fall

Standalone
The History of the United Kingdom
The History of Ireland
The History of America
Stalin
The Fiery Maelstrom of Freedom
The History of Scotland
Robert the Bruce
William Wallace: Scotland's Great Freedom Fighter
The History of Wales

www.ingramcontent.com/pod-product-compliance
Lightning Source LLC
Chambersburg PA
CBHW031748150726
47989CB00006B/2640